1,911
Best Things
Anybody
Ever Said

Also by Robert Byrne

*Cat Scan—All the Best
from the Literature of Cats*
(with Teressa Skelton)

1,911

Best Things
Anybody
Ever Said

Many amusingly illuminated
by antique etchings and line cuts

Robert Byrne

FAWCETT COLUMBINE · NEW YORK

A Fawcett Columbine Book
Published by Ballantine Books

Originally published in three volumes, as *The 637 Best Things Anybody Ever Said, The Other 637 Best Things Anybody Ever Said,* and *The Third and Possibly the Best 637 Best Things Anybody Ever Said.*

Library of Congress Catalog Card Number: 87-91869
ISBN: 0-449-90285-4
This edition published by arrangement with Atheneum Publishers, an imprint of Macmillan Publishing Company.

Cover design by James R. Harris
Text design by Mary A. Wirth

Manufactured in the United States of America
First Ballantine Books Trade Edition: October 1988
10

Thou shalt not steal.
Exodus 20:15
(ca. 700 B.C.*)*

Contents

1,911
Best Things
Anybody
Ever Said

Introduction

It's amazing how much wit, insight, and bile can be packed into a single short sentence. Look what Wilt Chamberlain, GARFIELD the Cat, and Alfred North Whitehead were able to say in only four words: "Nobody roots for Goliath." (Wilt); "Cute rots the intellect." (Garfield); "All truths are half-truths." (Al)

When Mort Sahl was asked to say something funny, he needed only three words to comply: "John Foster Dulles." It was the Roman poet Martial who pointed out that "Gifts are hooks." Somebody once said just as briefly that "Chaste makes waste."

Even two words sometimes suffice. Steven Pearl's suggested license-plate slogan for the State of New Jersey is "What died?" Or take a single word. When President Jimmy Carter's daughter Amy was a child, she was asked if she had any message for the children of America. "No," she said. Of course, the really short remarks usually require a setup, which detracts from their beauty. That's why the lines about gifts and chastity are so fine.

"I hate quotations," Ralph Waldo Emerson said in three words. "I don't," I reply in two. Quotations, aphorisms, epigrams, wisecracks, apothegms, call them what you will. I especially like them if . . . well, if they're the kind I especially like. It's hard to explain. Not only do I like them, I like telling them to other people, and if a friend isn't available I lie in wait for strangers.

The first sentence I ever uttered as an infant was a one-liner. At the age of eighteen months I pulled myself to my feet in my crib and said to my mother and father, "Call me a cab." They didn't do it, but they laughed, and the die was cast. I've been trying for the same reaction ever since. When my own words don't work I turn to the words of others.

After leaving the crib I started a notebook titled "Remarks Worth Remembering." It grew over the years and became a kind of jewel box of *bon mots*. I enjoyed leafing through it from time to time and feeling admiration, envy, and hatred for the authors. One day in 1981 it struck me that I had in my hands the basis for a unique book of quotations, one that would reflect my own tastes entirely. The collection I envisioned was all wheat and no chaff. It contained absolutely nothing inspirational, uplifting, or educational. Every entry was one a reader could use without being classed as a pompous fool. What a concept! Such a book would enable me to display my jewels to more strangers than I could shake a shtick at!

The result was *The 637 Best Things Anybody Ever Said*, which was originally published in 1982. The number 637 had no particular significance. It was simply the number of quotes remaining after I had boiled down my notebook and scavenged through the collections of others. Why not 638? I didn't want to pad it. Why not 636? I didn't want to leave any good ones out.

I didn't have high hopes for success in the marketplace. A slim volume of quotations can be expected to sink in the general flood of books, which pour from the nation's presses like noxious effluvia from a feed lot. Surprisingly, *The 637* was widely noticed by the media, maybe because all a reviewer had to do to fill a column was string together a bunch of quotes and go home early. It was gratifying to see that there was no agreement on which were the best lines.

A year later I had a problem. Sales justified a sequel, but what could it be called? Certainly not *The 637 Second-best Things Anybody Ever Said*. The first title had put me in a hole. There was no shortage of material for a follow up. Great lines were cropping up everywhere—in newspapers, magazines, movies, books, on television, during conversations, and in my mailbox. America is riddled with wags and wits, professional and amateur, and they never sleep. Lines I had missed the first time around cried out for a book of their own. A title for a sequel finally came to me, and in 1984 *The Other 637 Best Things Anybody Ever Said* was published in hardcover. I confessed in the introduction that in titling the earlier collection, I had lied.

Surely now I was done with the business, I thought, and could go back to writing novels. But no! The second book sold twice as many copies as the first, which meant that I got twice as many suggestions from readers. The moment I heard that Katherine Whitehorn had observed that outside every thin woman is a fat man trying to get in, I knew I had to go back into production. *The Third and Possibly the Best 637 Best Things Ever Said* came out in 1986.

One feature of the books is that, while related quotes are grouped by subject, the subjects aren't alphabetized. A typical sequence is Love, Sex, Marriage, Kids, Drink, Death, and Comedy, which, as you can see, tells a little story. In *The Third 637* Marriage follows Sex and Self-Abuse follows Marriage. In other quotation books, Sex is followed by such unrelated topics as Shakespeare, Sickness, and Socialism, and there is no category for Self-Abuse at all. Most collections of quotations strive for such things as comprehensiveness, balance, and fairness. Not this one. No attempt is made to include a quote for every topic or from every epoch.

Some quotations take on added point when their age is known. For that reason, and as a sop to scholars, I have included birth and death dates for historical figures. Where no dates are given, it can be assumed that the person is either still alive or only lately dead.

A word about ascriptions. "Unknown" is used when I have been unable to discover the source. Readers may be better informed. "Anonymous" is used when I am convinced that the source not only is unknown but is going to stay unknown. I'm uneasy about crediting lines to certain celebrities, for I sense the touch of the gag writer's hand. It would contribute to accuracy and completeness if those ghosts would step forward and identify themselves even if it costs them their jobs.

Some quotes are not numbered because they appeared earlier ("Plato was a bore."), and quotes used more than once are numbered on first appearance only ("Hemingway was a jerk.").

At the back of this omnibus edition you will find the sources, notes, and references for each of the three original books. You will also find indexes—covering the complete set —one for subjects and one for authors.

Finally, who, after all can say what is "best"? I can. So can you. What follows are my choices. Now it may be that you have heard, written, or read something that merits inclusion in a cream-of-the-crop collection like this but which is missing because for one reason or another you simply have never called it to my attention. Whose fault is that? I'm as close as your mailbox.

Have fun—I did.

Robert Byrne
c/o Fawcett Books
201 East 50th Street
New York, N.Y. 10022

The 637 Best Things Anybody Ever Said

Part I

God, Life, Death, Murder, Stupidity, Narcissism, Birth, Youth, Sex, Love, Marriage, Horses, Greeks, Romans, Politics, Literature, Drink, Presidents and a great deal more

1

Why don't you get a haircut? You look like a chrysanthe-
mum.   *P. G. Wodehouse (1881–1975)*

2

How can I believe in God when just last week I got my tongue
caught in the roller of an electric typewriter?

Woody Allen

3

If I had been present at creation, I would have given some
useful hints.   *Alfonso the Wise (1221–1284)*

4

The gods play games with men as balls.

Titus Maccius Platus (254?–184 B.C.)

5

He was a wise man who invented God.

Plato (427?–348? B.C.)

6

Plato is a bore.   *Nietzsche (1844–1900)*

7

It is the final proof of God's omnipotence that he need not exist in order to save us.

Peter De Vries

8

·Man is a god in ruins.

Ralph Waldo Emerson (1803–1882)

9

God has always been hard on the poor.

Jean Paul Marat (1743–1793)

10

Man is certainly stark mad. He cannot make a worm, and yet he will be making gods by dozens.

Montaigne (1553–1592)

11

The good Lord never gives you more than you can handle.
Unless you die of something.

Guindon cartoon caption

12

If I had been the Virgin Mary, I would have said "No."

Margaret "Stevie" Smith (1902–1971)

13

Few people can be happy unless they hate some other person, nation, or creed.

Bertrand Russell (1872–1970)

14

Religions change; beer and wine remain.

Hervey Allen (1889–1949)

15
The chicken probably came before the egg because it is hard to imagine God wanting to sit on an egg.

Unknown

16
In England there are sixty different religions and only one sauce. *Francesco Caracciolo (1752–1799)*

17
Living with a saint is more grueling than being one.

Robert Neville

18
He was of the faith chiefly in the sense that the church he currently did not attend was Catholic.

Kingsley Amis

19
Everybody should believe in something; I believe I'll have another drink. *Variously ascribed*

20
Under certain circumstances, profanity provides a relief denied even to prayer.

Mark Twain (1835–1910)

21

The trouble with born-again Christians is that they are an
even bigger pain the second time around.

Herb Caen

22

I'm astounded by people who want to "know" the universe
when it's hard enough to find your way around Chinatown.

Woody Allen

23

It is better to know some of the questions than all of the answers. *James Thurber (1894–1961)*

24

It is only possible to live happily ever after on a day to day basis. *Margaret Bonnano*

25

I have a new philosophy. I'm only going to dread one day at a time. *Charles Schulz*

26

I have a simple philosophy. Fill what's empty. Empty what's full. Scratch where it itches. *Alice Roosevelt Longworth (1884–1980)*

27

I know the answer! The answer lies within the heart of all mankind! The answer is twelve? I think I'm in the wrong building. *Charles Schulz*

28

Life is like an overlong drama through which we sit being nagged by the vague memories of having read the reviews. *John Updike*

29

There is more to life than increasing its speed.

Mahatma Gandhi (1869–1948)

30

Life is like playing a violin in public and learning the instrument as one goes on.

Samuel Butler (1835–1902)

31

Life is what happens while you are making other plans.

John Lennon (1940–1980)

32

Life is a God-damned, stinking, treacherous game and nine hundred and ninety-nine men out of a thousand are bastards.

Theodore Dreiser (1871–1945)
quoting an unnamed newspaper editor

33

There is no cure for birth and death save to enjoy the interval.   *George Santayana (1863–1952)*

34

Why is it that we rejoice at a birth and grieve at a funeral? It is because we are not the person involved.
                    Mark Twain (1835–1910)

35

The cost of living is going up and the chance of living is going down.   *Flip Wilson*

36

Is life worth living? That depends on the liver.
                    Unknown

37

Dying is one of the few things that can be done as easily lying down.   *Woody Allen*

38

I'm not afraid to die. I just don't want to be there when it happens.   *Woody Allen*

39

Perhaps there is no life after death . . . there's just Los Angeles.   *Rich Anderson*

40

Death is nature's way of saying "Howdy."

Unknown

41

The best way to get praise is to die.

Italian proverb

42

There is no such thing as inner peace. There is only nervousness and death.

Fran Lebowitz

43

In the long run we are all dead.

John Maynard Keynes (1883–1946)

44

The patient is not likely to recover who makes the doctor his heir.

Thomas Fuller (1608–1661)

45

After I'm dead I'd rather have people ask why I have no monument than why I have one.

Cato the Elder (234–149 B.C.)

46

For three days after death hair and fingernails continue to grow but phone calls taper off.

Johnny Carson

47

I wonder if anybody ever reached the age of thirty-five in New England without wanting to kill himself.

Barrett Wendell (1855–1921)

48

I have had just about all I can take of myself.

S. N. Behrman (1893–1973) on reaching the age of 75

49

When you don't have any money, the problem is food. When you have money, it's sex. When you have both, it's health. If everything is simply jake, then you're frightened of death.

J. P. Donleavy

50

Most people would sooner die than think; in fact, they do so.

Bertrand Russell (1872–1970)

51

Early one June morning in 1872 I murdered my father—an act which made a deep impression on me at the time.

Ambrose Bierce (1842–1914)

52

One murder makes a villain, millions a hero.

Beilby Porteus (1731–1808)

53

If once a man indulges himself in murder, very soon he comes to think little of robbing; and from robbing he next comes to drinking and Sabbath-breaking, and from that to incivility and procrastination.

Thomas De Quincey (1785–1859)

54

A murderer is one who is presumed to be innocent until proven insane.

Unknown

55

Either this man is dead or my watch has stopped.

Groucho Marx (1890–1977)

56

There is no money in poetry, but then there is no poetry in money, either.

Robert Graves

57

This poem will never reach its destination.

Voltaire (1694–1778) on Rousseau's Ode to Posterity

58

I hope that one or two immortal lyrics will come out of all this tumbling around.

*Poet Louise Bogan (1898–1970)
on her love affair with poet Theodore Roethke*

59

I write poetry not for publication but merely to kill time. Airplanes are a good place to write poetry and then firmly throw it away. My collected works are mostly on the vomit bags of Pan American and TWA.

Charles McCabe

60

The writing of more than 75 poems in any fiscal year should be punishable by a fine of $500.

Ed Sanders

61

Show me a poet and I'll show you a shit.

A. J. Liebling (1904–1963)

62

The human mind treats a new idea the way the body treats a strange protein; it rejects it.

Biologist P. B. Medawar

63

The intelligent man finds almost everything ridiculous, the sensible man hardly anything.

Goethe (1749–1832)

64

The difference between genius and stupidity is that genius has its limits.

Unknown

65

The only reason some people get lost in thought is because it's unfamiliar territory.   *Paul Fix*

66

Only the mediocre are always at their best.
                    Jean Giraudoux (1882–1944)

67

I'm going to speak my mind because I have nothing to lose.
                    S. I. Hayakawa

68

I live in the crowd of jollity, not so much to enjoy company as to shun myself.
                    Samuel Johnson (1709–1784)

69

For every ten jokes, thou hast got an hundred enemies.
                    Laurence Sterne (1713–1768)

70

Wit is educated insolence.
                    Aristotle (384–322 B.C.)

71

Seriousness is the only refuge of the shallow.
                    Oscar Wilde (1854–1900)

72

He who laughs, lasts.
                    Mary Pettibone Poole (c. 1938)

73

Man: An animal [whose] . . . chief occupation is extermination of other animals and his own species, which, however, multiplies with such insistent rapidity as to infest the whole habitable earth and Canada.

Ambrose Bierce (1842–1914)

74

Woman: An animal . . . having a rudimentary susceptibility to domestication . . . The species is the most widely distributed of all beasts of prey. . . . The woman is omnivorous and can be taught not to talk.

Ambrose Bierce (1842–1914)

75

Cabbage: A . . . vegetable about as large and wise as a man's head.
Ambrose Bierce (1842–1914)

76

Memorial Service: Farewell party for someone who has already left.
RB

77

Eunuch: A man who has had his works cut out for him.
RB

78

I hate definitions.
Benjamin Disraeli (1804–1881)

79

The affair between Margot Asquith and Margot Asquith will live as one of the prettiest love stories in all literature.
Dorothy Parker (1893–1967) in a review of a book by Margot Asquith

80
To love oneself is the beginning of a life-long romance.
Oscar Wilde (1854–1900)

81
Like all self-made men he worships his creator.

Unknown

82
Egotist: A person . . . more interested in himself than in me.

Ambrose Bierce (1842–1914)

83
A narcissist is someone better looking than you are.

Gore Vidal

84
Don't be humble. You're not that great.

Golda Meir (1898–1978)

85
Stop crime at its source! Support Planned Parenthood.

Robert Byrne

86
When turkeys mate they think of swans.

Johnny Carson

87
Except during the nine months before he draws his first breath, no man manages his affairs as well as a tree does.

George Bernard Shaw (1856–1950)

88

It is now quite lawful for a Catholic woman to avoid pregnancy by a resort to mathematics, though she is still forbidden to resort to physics or chemistry.

H. L. Mencken (1880–1956)

89

Somewhere on this globe, every ten seconds, there is a woman giving birth to a child. She must be found and stopped. *Sam Levenson (1911–1980)*

90

To enter life by way of the vagina is as good a way as any.
Henry Miller (1891–1980)

91

I have an intense desire to return to the womb. Anybody's.
Woody Allen

92

To my embarrassment I was born in bed with a lady.
Wilson Mizner (1876–1933)

93

My obstetrician was so dumb that when I gave birth he forgot to cut the cord. For a year that kid followed me *everywhere.* It was like having a dog on a leash.

Joan Rivers

94

I knew I was an unwanted baby when I saw that my bath toys were a toaster and a radio.

Joan Rivers

95

A child is a curly, dimpled lunatic.

Ralph Waldo Emerson (1803–1882)

96

All children are essentially criminal.

Denis Diderot (1713–1784)

97

A vegetarian is a person who won't eat anything that can have children.

David Brenner

98

When I was a child what I wanted to be when I grew up was an invalid.

Quentin Crisp

99

Children of the poor should work for some part of the day when they reach the age of three.

John Locke (1632–1704) in 1697

100

Of all the animals, the boy is the most unmanageable.

Plato (427?–348? B.C.)

Plato is a bore.

Nietzsche (1844–1900)

101

Children are guilty of unpardonable rudeness when they spit in the face of a companion; neither are they excusable who spit from windows or on walls or furniture.

St. John Baptist de La Salle (c. 1695)

102

Thank God kids never mean well.

Lily Tomlin

103

Mothers are fonder than fathers of their children because they are more certain they are their own.

Aristotle (384–322 B.C.)

104

There's nothing wrong with teenagers that reasoning with them won't aggravate. *Unknown*

105

Young people are more hopeful at a certain age than adults, but I suspect that's glandular. As for children, I keep as far from them as possible. I don't like the sight of them. The scale is all wrong. The heads tend to be too big for the bodies, and the hands and feet are a disaster. They keep falling into things. The nakedness of their bad character! We adults have learned how to disguise our terrible character, but children, well, they are like grotesque drawings of *us*. They should be neither seen nor heard, and no one must make another one. *Gore Vidal*

106

I tell you I can feel them! They're all around us! Young people! Getting closer and closer!

Hamilton cartoon caption

107

The reason husband and wives do not understand each other is because they belong to different sexes.

Dorothy Dix (1870–1951)

108

There was a time when we expected nothing of children but obedience, as opposed to the present, when we expect everything of them but obedience.

Anatole Broyard

109

The reason grandparents and grandchildren get along so well is that they have a common enemy.

Sam Levenson (1911–1980)

110

I never met a kid I liked.

W. C. Fields (1880–1946)

111

It is a good thing for an uneducated man to read books of quotations.   *Winston Churchill (1874–1965)*

112

I hate quotations.

Ralph Waldo Emerson (1803–1882)

113

If men could get pregnant, abortion would be a sacrament.

Florynce Kennedy

114

Ever since the young men have owned motorcycles, incest has been dying out.   *Max Frisch*

115

Familiarity breeds attempt.

Goodman Ace (1899–1982)

116

Sex drive: A physical craving that begins in adolescence and ends at marriage.   *Robert Byrne*

117
Sex is the most fun you can have without smiling.

Unknown

118
I would rather go to bed with Lillian Russell stark naked than Ulysses S. Grant in full military regalia.

Mark Twain (1835–1910)

119
Last time I tried to make love to my wife nothing was happening, so I said to her, "What's the matter, you can't think of anybody either?"

Rodney Dangerfield

120
If it weren't for pickpockets I'd have no sex life at all.

Rodney Dangerfield

121
I've tried several varieties of sex. The conventional position makes me claustrophobic and the others give me a stiff neck or lockjaw.

Tallulah Bankhead (1903–1968)

122
A woman occasionally is quite a serviceable substitute for masturbation.

Karl Kraus

123
Sex is nobody's business except the three people involved.
Unknown

124
What men desire is a virgin who is a whore.
Edward Dahlberg (1900–1977)

125
The orgasm has replaced the Cross as the focus of longing and the image of fulfillment.
Malcolm Muggeridge

126
All this fuss about sleeping together. For physical pleasure I'd sooner go to my dentist any day.
Evelyn Waugh (1903–1966)

127

What a man enjoys about a woman's clothes are his fantasies
of how she would look without them.

Brendan Francis

128

Women who miscalculate are called "mothers."

Abigail Van Buren

129
Nothing is so much to be shunned as sex relations.
St. Augustine (354–430)

130
I kissed my first girl and smoked my first cigarette on the same day. I haven't had time for tobacco since.
Arturo Toscanini (1867–1957)

131
The only really indecent people are the chaste.
J. K. Huysmans (1848–1907)

132
For the preservation of chastity, an empty and rumbling stomach and fevered lungs are indispensable.
St. Jerome (340?–420)

133
I hate women because they always know where things are.
James Thurber (1894–1961)

134
Sex is the biggest nothing of all time.
Andy Warhol

135

Love is the delightful interval between meeting a beautiful girl and discovering that she looks like a haddock.

John Barrymore (1882–1942)

136

Love is an ocean of emotions entirely surrounded by expenses.

Lord Dewar

137

Love is a grave mental disease.

Plato (427?–348? B.C.)

138

Whatever deceives seems to produce a magical enchantment.

Plato (427?–348? B.C.)

Plato is a bore.

Nietzsche (1844–1900)

139

The heaviest object in the world is the body of the woman you have ceased to love.
Marquis de Luc de Clapiers Vauvenargues (1715–1747)

140

In expressing love we belong among the undeveloped countries.   *Saul Bellow*

141

A man can be happy with any woman as long as he does not love her.   *Oscar Wilde (1854–1900)*

142

Love will find a lay.   *Robert Byrne*

143

It takes a woman twenty years to make a man of her son, and another woman twenty minutes to make a fool of him.
Helen Rowland (1876–1950)

144

It is better to have loved and lost than never to have lost at all.   *Samuel Butler (1835–1902)*

145

I sold my memoirs of my love life to Parker Brothers and they are going to make a game out of it.
Woody Allen

146

The only solid and lasting peace between a man and his wife
is doubtless a separation.

Lord Chesterfield (1694–1773)

147

Marriage: A master, a mistress and two slaves, making in all,
two. *Ambrose Bierce (1842–1914)*

148

Marriage is not a word but a sentence.

Unknown

149

Marriage is a great institution, but I'm not ready for an institution. *Mae West (1893–1980)*

150

If I ever marry it will be on a sudden impulse, as a man
shoots himself.

H. L. Mencken (1880–1956)

151

For the upper middle class, marriage is the only adventure
left. *Unknown*

152

We want playmates we can own.

Jules Feiffer on marriage

153

It was so cold I almost got married.

Shelley Winters

154

At American weddings, the quality of the food is inversely proportional to the social position of the bride and groom.

Calvin Trillin

155

I was married once. Now I just lease.

From the movie Buddy, Buddy *(1981)*

156

I married beneath me. All women do.

Nancy, Lady Astor (1879–1964)

157

An archeologist is the best husband a woman can have; the older she gets, the more interested he is in her.

Agatha Christie (1891–1976), who was married to one

158

I tended to place my wife under a pedestal.

Woody Allen

159

My mother-in-law broke up my marriage. One day my wife came home early from work and found us in bed together.

Lenny Bruce (1926–1966)

160

Divorce is the sacrament of adultery.

French proverb

161

What scares me about divorce is that my children might put me in a home for unwed mothers.

Teressa Skelton

162

Take my wife . . . please!

Henny Youngman

163

A Curse

May your soul be forever tormented by fire and your bones be dug up by dogs and dragged through the streets of Minneapolis.
Garrison Keillor

164

My work is done, why wait?
Suicide note left by Kodak founder George Eastman (1854–1932)

165
All right, then, I'll say it: Dante makes me sick.
Last words of Spanish playwright Lope de Vega on being
assured on his deathbed that the end was very near.

166
I don't feel good. *Last words of Luther Burbank*
(1849–1926)

167
Don't let it end like this. Tell them I said something.
Last words of Pancho Villa (1877?–1923)

168
It is better to be a coward for a minute than dead for the rest
of your life. *Irish proverb*

169
The reverse side also has a reverse side.
Japanese proverb

170
Tell the truth and run.
Yugoslavian proverb

171
Do not insult the mother alligator until after you have
crossed the river. *Haitian proverb*

172
Too clever is dumb.
German proverb

173

The Irish ignore anything they can't drink or punch.

Old saying

174

If God lived on earth, people would break his windows.

Jewish proverb

175

It is nothing, they are only thrashing my husband.

Portuguese proverb

176

When the cat and mouse agree, the grocer is ruined.

Persian proverb

177

I do not say a proverb is amiss when aptly and reasonably applied, but to be forever discharging them, right or wrong, hit or miss, renders conversation insipid and vulgar.

Miguel Cervantes (1547–1616)

178

Wise men make proverbs but fools repeat them.

Samuel Palmer (c. 1710)

179

Nobody has ever bet enough on the winning horse.

Overheard at a track by Richard Sasuly

180

One of the worst things that can happen in life is to win a bet on a horse at an early age.

Danny McGoorty (1901–1970)

181

Nobody ever committed suicide who had a good two-year-old in the barn.

Racetrack proverb

182

It is morally wrong to allow suckers to keep their money.

"Canada Bill" Jones

183

All life is six to five against.

Damon Runyon (1884–1946)

184

Much as he is opposed to lawbreaking, he is not bigoted about it.

Damon Runyon (1884–1946)

185

You might as well fall flat on your face as lean over too far
backward.   *James Thurber (1894–1961)*

186

Alexander III of Macedonia is known as Alexander the Great
because he killed more people of more different kinds than
any other man of his time.

Will Cuppy (1884–1949)

187

Aristotle was famous for knowing everything. He taught that
the brain exists merely to cool the blood and is not involved
in the process of thinking. This is true only of certain per-
sons.   *Will Cuppy (1884–1949)*

188

All Gaul is divided into three parts: igneous, metamorphic,
and sedimentary.

Geologist Wilson Hinckley (1928–1972)

189

What a time! What a civilization!

Cicero (106–43 B.C.)

190

Oh, this age! How tasteless and ill-bred it is!

Catullus (87?–54? B.C.)

191

How little you know about the age you live in if you think that
honey is sweeter than cash in hand.

Ovid (43? B.C.–A.D. *18) ·*

192

It is sometimes expedient to forget who we are.

Publilius Syrus (c. 42 B.C.)

193

There is no glory in outstripping donkeys.

Martial (40–102)

194

The school of hard knocks is an accelerated curriculum.

Menander (342?–292? B.C.)

195

There is nothing so absurd but some philosopher has said
it.   *Cicero (106–43 B.C.)*

196

A man with his belly full of the classics is an enemy of the
human race.   *Henry Miller (1891–1980)*

197

Patriotism is the willingness to kill and be killed for trivial
reasons.   *Bertrand Russell (1872–1970)*

198

Democracy substitutes election by the incompetent many for appointment by the corrupt few.

George Bernard Shaw (1856–1950)

199

American has been discovered before, but it has always been hushed up.

Oscar Wilde (1854–1900)

200

The 100% American is 99% an idiot.

George Bernard Shaw (1856–1950)

201

A government which robs Peter to pay Paul can always depend on the support of Paul.

George Bernard Shaw (1856–1950)

202

And that's the world in a nutshell—an appropriate receptacle.

Stan Dunn

203

The remarkable thing about Shakespeare is that he really is very good, in spite of all the people who say he is very good.

Robert Graves

204

Crude, immoral, vulgar, and senseless.

Tolstoy (1882–1910) on Shakespeare

205

I know not, sir, whether Bacon wrote the works of Shakespeare, but if he did not it seems to me that he missed the opportunity of his life.

J. M. Barrie (1860–1937)

206

If Shakespeare had been in pro basketball he never would have had time to write his soliloquies. He would always have been on a plane between Phoenix and Kansas City.

Paul Westhead, basketball coach

207

A team is a team is a team. Shakespeare said that many times.

Dan Devine, football coach

208

A piano is a piano is a piano.—Gertrude Steinway

Unknown

209

A manuscript, like a foetus, is never improved by showing it to somebody before it is completed.

Unknown

210

Every journalist has a novel in him, which is an excellent place for it.   *Russell Lynes*

211

Why authors write I do not know. As well ask why a hen lays an egg or a cow stands patiently while a farmer burglarizes her.   *H. L. Mencken (1880–1956)*

212

Why do writers write? Because it isn't there.

Thomas Berger

213

Never let a domestic quarrel ruin a day's writing. If you can't start the next day fresh, get rid of your wife.

One of Mario Puzo's rules for writing a best-selling novel

214

Every novel should have a beginning, a muddle, and an end.

Peter De Vries

215

Boy meets girl; girl gets boy into pickle; boy gets pickle into girl.   *Jack Woodford (1894–1971) on plotting*

216

Writing is easy. All you do is stare at a blank sheet of paper until drops of blood form on your forehead.

Gene Fowler (1890–1960)

217

With a novelist, like a surgeon, you have to get a feeling that you've fallen into good hands—someone from whom you can accept the anesthetic with confidence.

Saul Bellow

218

Sometimes when reading Goethe I have a paralyzing suspicion that he is trying to be funny.

Guy Davenport

219

The novelist, afraid his ideas may be foolish, slyly puts them in the mouth of some other fool and reserves the right to disavow them.

Diane Johnson

220

He can compress the most words into the smallest idea of any man I ever met.

Abraham Lincoln (1809–1865)

221

If a writer has to rob his mother he will not hesitate; the *Ode On a Grecian Urn* is worth any number of old ladies.

William Faulkner (1897–1962)

222

In literature as in love, we are astonished at what is chosen by others.   *André Maurois (1885–1967)*

223

It is a delicious thing to write, to be no longer yourself but to move in an entire universe of your own creating. Today, for instance, as man and woman, both lover and mistress, I rode in a forest on an autumn afternoon under the yellow leaves, and I was also the horses, the leaves, the wind, the words my people uttered, even the red sun that made them almost close their love-drowned eyes. When I brood over these marvelous pleasures I have enjoyed, I would be tempted to offer God a prayer of thanks if I knew he could hear me. Praised may he be for not creating me a cotton merchant, a vaudevillian, or a wit.

Gustave Flaubert (1821–1880)

224

I'm a lousy writer; a helluva lot of people have got lousy taste.
Grace Metalious (1924–1964)

225

A custom loathsome to the eye, hateful to the nose, harmful to the brain, dangerous to the lungs, and in the black, stinking fumes thereof, nearest resembling the horrible Stygian smoke of the pit that is bottomless.

King James (c. 1604) on smoking

226

I can write better than anybody who can write faster, and I can write faster than anybody who can write better.
A. J. Liebling (1904–1963)

227

I used to be treated like an idiot, now I'm treated like an idiot savant. *Martin Cruz Smith after his novel* Gorky Park *became a best-seller*

228

Income tax returns are the most imaginative fiction being written today. *Herman Wouk*

229

Marry money.

Max Shulman's advice to aspiring authors

230

What is a writer but a shmuck with an Underwood?

Jack Warner (ascribed)

231

There's no thief like a bad book.

Italian proverb

232

A big book is a big bore.

Callimachus (c. 260 B.C.)

233

Never read a book that is not a year old.

Ralph Waldo Emerson (1803–1882)

234

The man who doesn't read good books has no advantage over the man who can't read them.

Mark Twain (1835–1910)

235

Any ordinary man can . . . surround himself with two thousand books . . . and thenceforward have at least one place in the world in which it is possible to be happy.

Augustine Birrell (1850–1933)

236

I have always imagined that Paradise will be a kind of library.

Jorge Luis Borges

237

Studying literature at Harvard is like learning about women at the Mayo Clinic.

Roy Blount, Jr.

238

I wonder how so insupportable a thing as a bookseller was ever permitted to grow up in the Commonwealth. Many of our modern booksellers are but needless excrements, or rather vermin.

George Wither (1588–1667)

239

It takes the publishing industry so long to produce books it's no wonder so many are posthumous.

Teressa Skelton

240

In every fat book there is a thin book trying to get out.

Unknown

241

No, I haven't read the New Testament, but I read the Old Testament, and I liked it very, very much.

One shepherd to another in a New Yorker *cartoon*

242

What an ugly beast is the ape, and how like us.

Cicero (106–43 B.C.)

243
Your life story would not make a good book. Don't even try.

Fran Lebowitz

244
Drunkenness is the ruin of reason. It is premature old age. It is temporary death.

St. Basil (330?–379?)

245
I drink no more than a sponge.

Rabelais (1494–1553)

246
They talk of my drinking but never my thirst.

Scottish proverb

247
A drinker has a hole under his nose that all his money runs into.

Thomas Fuller (1608–1661)

248
'Twas a woman who drove me to drink, and I never had the courtesy to thank her for it.

W. C. Fields (1880–1946)

249

An Irishman is the only man in the world who will step over the bodies of a dozen naked women to get to a bottle of stout.   *Unknown*

250

One more drink and I'll be under the host.
                                        Dorothy Parker (1893–1967)

251

I drink to make other people more interesting.
                                        George Jean Nathan (1882–1958)

252

Inflation has gone up over a dollar a quart.
                                        W. C. Fields (1880–1946)

253

Even though a number of people have tried, no one has yet found a way to drink for a living.

                                        Jean Kerr

254

I haven't touched a drop of alcohol since the invention of the funnel.   *Malachy McCourt*

255

The less I behave like Whistler's mother the night before, the more I look like her the morning after.

Tallulah Bankhead (1903–1968)

256

One reason I don't drink is that I want to know when I am having a good time.

Nancy, Lady Astor (1879–1964)

257

I'd rather have a free bottle in front of me than a prefrontal lobotomy.   *Tom Waits*

258

I hate to advocate drugs, alcohol, violence, or insanity to anyone, but they've always worked for me.

Hunter S. Thompson

259

If you drink, don't drive. Don't even putt.

Dean Martin

260

I tremble for my country when I reflect that God is just.
Thomas Jefferson (1743-1826)

261

If you weren't such a great man you'd be a terrible bore.
Mrs. William Gladstone to her husband

262

He speaks to me as if I were a public meeting.
Queen Victoria (1819-1901) on Gladstone

263

Harding was not a bad man, he was just a slob.
Alice Roosevelt Longworth (1884-1980)

264

The only man, woman, or child who ever wrote a simple declarative sentence with seven grammatical errors is dead.
e. e. cummings (1894-1962) on the death of Warren G. Harding, 1923

265

In 1932, lame duck President Herbert Hoover was so desperate to remain in the White House that he dressed up as Eleanor Roosevelt. When FDR discovered the hoax in 1936, the two men decided to stay together for the sake of the children.
Johnny Carson

266

The Arabs are a backward people who eat nothing but camel dung.   *Winston Churchill (1874–1965)*

267

Things have never been more like the way they are today in history.

Dwight David Eisenhower (1890–1969)

268

John Foster Dulles.   *Mort Sahl on being asked to say something funny*

269

Listen, there is no courage or any extra courage that I know of to find out the right thing to do. Now, it is not only necessary to do the right thing, but to do it in the right way and the only problem you have is what is the right thing to do and what is the right way to do it. That is the problem. But this economy of ours is not so simple that it obeys to the opinion of bias or the pronouncements of any particular individual, even to the President. This is an economy that is made up of 173 million people and it reflects their desires, they're ready to buy, they're to spend, it is a thing that is too complex and too big to be affected adversely or advantageously just by a few words or any particular—say, a little this and that, or even a panacea so alleged.

Dwight David Eisenhower (1890–1969) in response to the question: "Has government been lacking in courage and boldness in facing up to the recession?"

270

Nixon is a shifty-eyed goddamn liar. . . . He's one of the few in the history of this country to run for high office talking out of both sides of his mouth at the same time and lying out of both sides.   *Harry S Truman (1884–1972)*

271

I don't give a shit about the Italian lira.

*President Richard M. Nixon
on being asked by H. R. Haldeman if he wanted to hear
a report on the decline of the Italian lira.*

272

I would have made a good Pope.

Richard M. Nixon

273

How do you like that guy? Can't run six balls and he's President of the United States.   *Pool hustler Johnny Irish
on Nixon*

274

Henry Kissinger may have wished I had presented him as a combination of Charles DeGaulle and Disraeli, but I didn't . . . out of respect for DeGaulle and Disraeli. I described him as a cowboy because that is how he described himself. If I were a cowboy I would be offended.

Oriana Fallaci

275

Gerry Ford is a nice guy, but he played too much football with his helmet off.

Lyndon Baines Johnson (1908–1973)

276

I never trust a man unless I've got his pecker in my pocket.

Lyndon Baines Johnson (1908–1973)

277

No.   *President Jimmy Carter's daughter Amy when asked by a reporter if she had any message for the children of America.*

278

Sometimes when I look at my children I say to myself, "Lillian, you should have stayed a virgin."

Lillian Carter, mother of Jimmy and Billy

279

"Who's Virginia?"   *Rose Kennedy when asked why her daughter-in-law Joan lived in Boston while her son Ted lived in Virginia.*

280

I see the world in very fluid, contradictory, emerging, interconnected terms, and with that kind of circuitry I just don't feel the need to say what is going to happen or will not happen.   *California Governor Jerry Brown*

281

Ronald Reagan is not a typical politician because he doesn't know how to lie, cheat, and steal. He's always had an agent for that.   *Bob Hope*

282

Ronald Reagan is the Fred Astaire of foot-in-mouth disease.
Jeff Davis

283

Never forget that the most powerful force on earth is love.
Nelson Rockefeller (1908–1979) to Henry Kissinger

284

Sure Reagan promised to take senility tests. But what if he forgets?   *Lorna Kerr-Walker*

285

Ronald Reagan is the most ignorant president since Warren Harding.   *Ralph Nader*

286

Ronald Reagan has held the two most demeaning jobs in the country—President of the United States and radio broadcaster for the Chicago Cubs.

George Will

287

Nancy Reagan fell down and broke her hair.

Johnny Carson

288

Well, I would—if they realized that we—again if—if we led them back to that stalemate only because that our retaliatory power, our seconds, or strike at them after our first strike, would be so destructive that they couldn't afford it, that would hold them off.

Ronald Reagan when asked if nuclear war could be limited to tactical weapons.

289

Nixon, Ford, Carter, Reagan—a Mount Rushmore of incompetence.　*David Steinberg*

290

When I was a boy I was told that anybody could become President; I'm beginning to believe it.

Clarence Darrow (1857–1938)

291

I'd rather entrust the government of the United States to the first 400 people listed in the Boston telephone directory than to the faculty of Harvard University.

William F. Buckley, Jr.

292

The only thing that saves us from the bureaucracy is its inefficiency.　*Eugene McCarthy*

293

We have a crisis of leadership in this country. Where are the Washingtons, the Jeffersons, and the Jacksons? I'll tell you where they are—they are playing professional football and basketball. *Unknown*

294

It is inaccurate to say I hate everything. I am strongly in favor of common sense, common honesty, and common decency. This makes me forever ineligible for any public office.
H. L. Mencken (1880–1956)

295

What this country needs is more unemployed politicians.
Edward Langley

296

All right, I will learn to read, but when I have learned, I never, never shall. *British novelist David Garnett at age 4, to his mother*

297

Henry James writes fiction as if it were a painful duty.
Oscar Wilde (1854–1900)

298

Henry James chews more than he bites off.
Mrs. Henry Adams (c. 1880)

299
Henry James was one of the nicest old ladies I ever met.
William Faulkner (1897–1962)

300
Henry James would have been vastly improved as a novelist by a few whiffs of the Chicago stockyards.
H. L. Mencken (1880–1956)

301
Henry James created more convincing women than Iris Murdoch put together.
Wilfred Sheed

302
Go not in and out of court that thy name may not stink.
The Wisdom of Anii (c. 900 B.C.)

303
A lawyer and a wagon-wheel must be well greased.
German proverb

304
Law is a bottomless pit.
John Arbuthnot (1667–1735) (c. 1712)

305

Lawyers, I suppose, were children once.

Charles Lamb (1775-1834)

306

When men are pure, laws are useless; when men are corrupt, laws are broken.

Benjamin Disraeli (1804-1881)

307

I became a policeman because I wanted to be in a business where the customer is always wrong.

Unnamed officer quoted by Arlene Heath

308

The mistakes are all there waiting to be made.

Chessmaster Savielly Grigorievitch Tartakower (1887-1956) on the game's opening position.

309

Moral victories don't count.

Savielly Grigorievitch Tartakower (1887-1956)

310

The only reason I would take up jogging is so that I could hear heavy breathing again.

Erma Bombeck

311

I don't jog. If I die I want to be sick.

Abe Lemons

312

It was such a primitive country we didn't even see any joggers.

Hamilton cartoon caption

313

Be careful about reading health books. You may die of a misprint.

Mark Twain (1835–1910)

314

Old people shouldn't eat health foods. They need all the preservatives they can get.

Robert Orben

315

A closed mouth gathers no feet.

Unknown

Part II

Miscellaneous

316

Never eat more than you can lift.

Miss Piggy

317

Punctuality is the thief of time.

Oscar Wilde (1854–1900)

318

Platitudes are the Sundays of stupidity.

Unknown

319

It is unbecoming for young men to utter maxims.

Aristotle (384–322 B.C.)

320

They were such a progressive couple they tried to adopt a gay baby. *Unknown*

321

He who marries a widow will often have a dead man's head thrown in his dish. *Spanish proverb*

322

I don't know the key to success, but the key to failure is trying to please everybody.

Bill Cosby

323

The brain is a wonderful organ; it starts working the moment you get up in the morning and does not stop until you get to the office.   *Robert Frost (1874–1963)*

324

I have never seen a greater monster or miracle than myself.
Montaigne (1533–1592)

325

Until you walk a mile in another man's moccasins you can't imagine the smell.   *Robert Byrne*

326

I don't have a warm personal enemy left. They've all died off. I miss them terribly because they helped define me.
Claire Boothe Luce

327

I'm lonesome. They are all dying. I have hardly a warm personal enemy left.
James McNeill Whistler (1834–1903)

328

Nothing is said that has not been said before.
Terence (185–159 B.C.)

329

I'm in a phone booth at the corner of Walk and Don't Walk.

Unknown

330

How come they picked you to be an astronaut? You got such a great sense of direction?

Jackie Mason

331

Recipe (in its entirety) for boiled owl:
Take feathers off. Clean owl and put in cooking pot with lots of water. Add salt to taste.

The Eskimo Cookbook *(1952)*

332

Do not make loon soup.

Valuable advice from The Eskimo Cookbook

333
Fall is my favorite season in Los Angeles, watching the birds change color and fall from the trees.

David Letterman

334
I met a guy once who was half Italian and half Chinese. His name was Video Pong.

Unknown

335
My father never lived to see his dream come true of an all-Yiddish-speaking Canada.

David Steinberg

336
That man has missed something who has never left a brothel at sunrise feeling like throwing himself into the river out of pure disgust.

Gustave Flaubert (1821–1880)

337
Gary Cooper and Greta Garbo may be the same person. Have you ever seen them together?

Ernst Lubitsch (1892–1947)

338
He had a God-given killer instinct.

Al Davis of the Oakland Raiders on George Blanda

339

I was gratified to be able to answer promptly. I said I don't know.

Mark Twain (1835–1910)

340

Few people know how to be old.

La Rochefoucauld (1613–1680)

341

The enemy came. He was beaten. I am tired. Goodnight.

*Message sent by Vicomte Turenne
after the battle of Dunen, 1658*

342

Byrne's Law: In any electrical circuit, appliances and wiring will burn out to protect fuses.

Robert Byrne

343

McCabe's Law: Nobody *has* to do *anything*.

Charles McCabe

344

Parker's Law: Beauty is only skin deep, but ugly goes clear to the bone.

from Murphy's Law

345

Chamberlain's Law: Everything tastes more or less like chicken.

from The Official Rules

346

A man can wear a hat for years without being oppressed by its shabbiness. *James Douglas*

347

Boozer's Revision: A bird in the hand is dead.
from The Official Rules

348

Any fool can make a rule.
Henry David Thoreau (1817–1862)

349

Happiness Is Seeing Lubbock, Texas, in the Rearview Mirror.
Song title

350

The important thing in acting is to be able to laugh and cry.
If I have to cry, I think of my sex life. If I have to laugh, I think
of my sex life. *Glenda Jackson*

351

There are more bores around than when I was a boy.
Fred Allen (1894–1956)

352

I've tried relaxing, but—I don't know—I feel more comforta-
ble tense. *Hamilton cartoon caption*

353

I'm just a person trapped inside a woman's body.
Elayne Boosler

354

I happened to catch my reflection the other day when I was
polishing my trophies, and, gee, it's easy to see why women
are nuts about me. *Tom Ryan*

355

What to do in case of emergency:
1. Pick up your hat
2. Grab your coat
3. Leave your worries on the doorstep
4. Direct your feet to the sunny side of the street.

Unknown

356

Nolan Ryan is pitching much better now that he has his curve ball straightened out.

Joe Garagiola

357

In many ways the saying "Know thyself" is lacking. Better to know other people.

Menander (342?–292? B.C.)

358

Only the shallow know themselves.

Oscar Wilde (1854–1900)

359

We all have the strength to endure the misfortunes of others.

La Rochefoucauld (1613–1680)

360

There is no sweeter sound than the crumbling of one's fellow man.

Groucho Marx (1890–1977)

361

It takes a great man to make a good listener.

Arthur Helps (1813–1875)

362

In this business you either sink or swim or you don't.

David Snell

363

I don't have a photograph, but you can have my footprints. They're upstairs in my socks.

Groucho Marx (1890–1977)

364

I've always been interested in people, but I've never liked them.

W. Somerset Maugham (1874–1965)

365

Are you going to come quietly or do I have to use earplugs?
From The Goon Show

366

One of the symptoms of an approaching nervous breakdown is the belief that one's work is terribly important.
Bertrand Russell (1872–1970)

367

A little inaccuracy sometimes saves tons of explanation.
H. H. Munro (Saki) (1870–1916)

368

It's really hard to be roommates with people if your suitcases are much better than theirs.
J. D. Salinger

369

Take most people, they're crazy about cars. I'd rather have a goddamn horse. A horse is at least *human,* for God's sake.
J. D. Salinger

370

Three o'clock is always too late or too early for anything you want to do.
Jean-Paul Sartre (1905–1980)

371

A reformer is a guy who rides through a sewer in a glass-bottomed boat.

New York Mayor Jimmy Walker (1881–1946) in 1928

372

The doctor can bury his mistakes but an architect can only advise his client to plant vines.

Frank Lloyd Wright (1869–1959)

373

I wash everything on the gentle cycle. It's much more humane.

Unknown.

374

The breakfast of champions is not cereal, it's the opposition.

Nick Seitz

375

There is nothing in the world so enjoyable as a thoroughgoing monomania.

Agnes Repplier (1858–1950)

376

Virtue is its own revenge.

E. Y. Harburg (1898–1981)

377

A good deed never goes unpunished.

Gore Vidal

378
The curtain rises on a vast primitive wasteland, not unlike certain parts of New Jersey.

Woody Allen

379

Man is the only animal that laughs and has a state legislature.
Samuel Butler (1835–1902)

380

Until a child is one year old it is incapable of sin.
The Talmud (c. 200)

381

I wish people who have trouble communicating would just shut up. *Tom Lehrer*

382

A man is as young as the woman he feels.
Variously ascribed

383

Toots Shor's restaurant is so crowded nobody goes there anymore. *Yogi Berra*

384

I don't care what is written about me so long as it isn't true.
Dorothy Parker (1893–1967)

385

He can beat yourn with hisn and he can beat hisn with yourn. *Pro football coach "Bum" Phillips on the merits of coach Don Shula*

386

More than any time in history mankind faces a crossroads. One path leads to despair and utter hopelessness, the other to total extinction. Let us pray that we have the wisdom to choose correctly.   *Woody Allen*

387

It is dangerous to be sincere unless you are also stupid.
George Bernard Shaw (1856–1950)

388

You can't steal second base and keep one foot on first.
An unnamed 60-year-old junior executive

389

When something good happens it's a miracle and you should wonder what God is saving up for you later.
Marshall Brickman

390

Cogito ergo spud. I think, therefore I yam.

Graffito

391

If you want an audience, start a fight.

Gaelic proverb

392

Everything hurts.   *Michaelangelo Antonioni*

393

I propose getting rid of conventional armaments and replacing them with reasonably priced hydrogen bombs that would be distributed equally throughout the world.

Idi Amin

394

I like a woman with a head on her shoulders. I hate necks.

Steve Martin

395

I don't know why people like the home run so much. A home run is over as soon as it starts . . . wham, bam, thank you, ma'am. The triple is the most exciting play of the game. A triple is like meeting a woman who excites you, spending the evening talking and getting more excited, then taking her home. It drags on and on. You're never sure how it's going to turn out.   *Baseball player George Foster*

396

Working on television is like being shot out of a cannon. They cram you all up with rehearsals, then someone lights a fuse and—BANG—there you are in someone's living room.
    Tallulah Bankhead (1903–1968)

397

Talk is cheap because supply exceeds demand.
    Unknown

398

Fifteen cents of every twenty-cent stamp goes for storage.
    Louis Rukeyser

399

The unique thing about Margaret Rutherford is that she can act with her chin alone. Among its many moods I especially cherish the chin commanding, the chin in doubt, and the chin at bay.   *Kenneth Tynan*

400

Things are so bad on Broadway today an actor is lucky to be miscast.   *George S. Kaufman (1889–1961)*

401

The race may not be to the swift nor the victory to the strong, but that's how you bet.

Damon Runyon (1844–1946)

402

The Jewish position on abortion is that a foetus is a foetus until it gets out of medical school.

Unknown

403

I'm impressed with people from Chicago. Hollywood is hype, New York is talk, Chicago is work.

Actor-producer Michael Douglas

404

An empty taxi stopped, and Jack Warner got out.

Unknown

405

A liberated woman is one who has sex before marriage and a job after.   *Gloria Steinem*

406

If you haven't got anything nice to say about anybody, come sit next to me.

Alice Roosevelt Longworth (1884–1980)

407

I'll try anything once.

Alice Roosevelt Longworth (1884–1980)
on giving birth at age 41.

408

Days off.

Spencer Tracy (1900–1967)
when asked what he looks for in a script.

409

We are drawn to our television sets each April the way we are drawn to the scene of an accident.

Vincent Canby on the Academy Awards

410

God sends meat and the devil sends cooks.

Thomas Deloney (1543–1600)

411

Husbands are like fires. They go out if unattended.

Zsa Zsa Gabor (Miss Hungary of 1936)

412
Go, and never darken my towels again.

Groucho Marx (1895–1977)

413
California is the only state in the union where you can fall
asleep under a rose bush in full bloom and freeze to death.

W. C. Fields (1880–1946)

414

The difference between Los Angeles and yoghurt is that yoghurt has an active, living culture.

Unknown

415

We can see California coming, and we're scared.

James Brady

416

Many a man owes his success to his first wife and his second wife to his success.

Jim Backus

417

Nature has given us two ears but only one mouth.

Benjamin Disraeli (1804–1881)

418

It is easier to stay out than get out.

Mark Twain (1835–1910)

419

A fat paunch never breeds fine thoughts.

St. Jerome (340?–420)

420

Absence makes the heart go yonder.

RB

421

Short, balding, Chinese gentleman seeks tall Negress with passion for leather and Brahms to attend openings.

Classified ad in the Berkeley Barb

422

Yard sale—Recently married couple is combining households. All duplicates will be sold, except children.

Classified ad in the San Jose Mercury News

423

It takes two to speak the truth—one to speak and another to hear.

Henry David Thoreau (1817–1862)

424

Only sick music makes money today.

Nietzsche (1844–1900) in 1888

425

I never know how much of what I say is true.

Bette Midler

426

I'm as pure as the driven slush.

Tallulah Bankhead (1903–1968)

427

I went around the world last year and you want to know something? It hates each other.

Edward J. Mannix

428

A great many people have come up to me and asked how I managed to get so much done and still look so dissipated.

Robert Benchley (1889–1945)

429

I don't trust him. We're friends.

Bertolt Brecht (1898–1956)

430

A man can't be too careful in the choice of his enemies.

Oscar Wilde (1854–1900)

431

Anyone can win, unless there happens to be a second entry.

George Ade (1866–1944)

432

We have long passed the Victorian era, when asterisks were followed after a certain interval by a baby.

W. Somerset Maugham (1874–1965)

433

It was such a lovely day I thought it was a pity to get up.

W. Somerset Maugham (1874–1965)

434

The biggest sin is sitting on your ass.

Florynce Kennedy

435

Laugh and the world laughs with you, snore and you sleep alone.

Anthony Burgess

436

It was a blonde, a blonde to make a bishop kick a hole in a stained glass window.

Raymond Chandler (1888–1959)

437

I go to the theater to be entertained . . . I don't want to see rape, sodomy, and drug addiction. I can get all that at home.

Roger Law cartoon caption

438

The higher the buildings, the lower the morals.
Noel Coward (1899–1973)

439

Nothing is illegal if a hundred businessmen decide to do it.
Andrew Young

440

I wish Frank Sinatra would just shut up and sing.
Lauren Bacall

441

England produces the best fat actors.
Jimmy Cannon (1910–1973)

442

If it weren't for Philo T. Farnsworth, inventor of television, we'd still be eating frozen radio dinners.

Johnny Carson

443

A luxury liner is just a bad play surrounded by water.

Clive James

444

The future isn't what it used to be. *Variously ascribed*

445

Some of us are becoming the men we wanted to marry.

Gloria Steinem

446

I haven't been wrong since 1961, when I thought I made a mistake. *Bob Hudson*

447

I may have my faults, but being wrong ain't one of them.

Jimmy Hoffa (1913–1975)

448

He had a winning smile, but everything else was a loser.

George C. Scott at a Bob Hope roast

449

He not only overflowed with learning, he stood in the slop.
Sydney Smith (1771–1845) on Macaulay

450

Listening to the Fifth Symphony of Ralph Vaughan Williams is like staring at a cow for forty-five minutes.
Aaron Copland

451

Forgive your enemies, but never forget their names.
John F. Kennedy (1917–1963)

452

There is no pleasure in having nothing to do; the fun is having lots to do and not doing it.
John W. Raper

453

Hope is the feeling you have that the feeling you have isn't permanent.
Jean Kerr

454

I was probably the only revolutionary ever referred to as "cute."
Abbie Hoffman

455

Success didn't spoil me; I've always been insufferable.
Fran Lebowitz

456

Men should stop fighting among themselves and start fighting insects.   *Luther Burbank (1849–1926)*

457

They say you can't do it, but sometimes it doesn't always work.   *Casey Stengel (1891–1975)*

458

Tumescence is the period between pubescence and senescence.   *Robert Byrne*

459

If this is coffee, please bring me some tea; but if this is tea, please bring me some coffee.

Abraham Lincoln (1809–1865)

460
Logic is in the eye of the logician.

Gloria Steinem

461
Everything is in a state of flux, including the status quo.

Robert Byrne

462
The only people with a right to complain about what I do for a living are vegetarian nudists.

Ken Bates, one of California's 700 licensed fur trappers

463
I'm trying to arrange my life so that I don't even have to be present. *Unknown*

464
To travel is to discover that everyone is wrong about other countries. *Aldous Huxley (1894–1963)*

465
It can be great fun to have an affair with a bitch.

Louis Auchincloss

466
Never accept a drink from a urologist.

Erma Bombeck's father

467
In Rome I am weighed down by a lack of momentum, the inertia of a spent civilization. In New York I feel plugged into a strong alternating current of hope and despair.

Ted Morgan

468
I'm six foot eleven. My birthday covers three days.

Darryl Dawkins

469
He who hesitates is not only lost, but miles from the next exit.

Unknown

470

You can't measure time in days the way you can money in dollars because every day is different.

Jorge Luis Borges

471

Time is nature's way of keeping everything from happening at once.

Unknown

472

If Today Was a Fish, I'd Throw It Back In.

Song title

473

From the Gutter to You Ain't Up.

Song title

474

I look at ordinary people in their suits, them with no scars, and I'm different. I don't fit with them. I'm where everybody's got scar tissue on their eyes and got noses like saddles. I go to conventions of old fighters like me and I see the scar tissue and all them flat noses and it's beautiful. Galento, may he rest in peace. Giardello, LaMotta, Carmen Basilio. What a sweetheart Basilio is. They talk like me, like they got rocks in their throats. Beautiful!

Willie Pastrano

475

Reality is a crutch for people who can't cope with drugs.

Lily Tomlin

476

A cap of good acid costs five dollars and for that you can hear the Universal Symphony with God singing solo and the Holy Ghost on drums.

Hunter S. Thompson as quoted by William F. Buckley, Jr., who added: "Though one should be prepared to vomit rather frequently and disport with pink elephants and assorted grotesqueries while trying, often unsuccessfully, to make one's way to the toilet."

477

The best way to lose weight is to get the flu and take a trip to Egypt. *Roz Lawrence*

478

Anyone who eats three meals a day should understand why cookbooks outsell sex books three to one.

L. M. Boyd

479

We don't know a millionth of one percent about anything.

Thomas Alva Edison (1847–1931)

480

Something ignoble, loathsome, undignified attends all associations between people and has been transferred to all objects, dwellings, tools, even the landscape itself.

Bertolt Brecht (1898–1956) on America

481

If I had known I was going to live this long I would have taken better care of myself.   *Unknown*

482

Is sloppiness in speech caused by ignorance or apathy? I don't know and I don't care.

William Safire

483

We had seen the light at the end of the tunnel, and it was out.

John C. Clancy

484

To err is human, to forgive supine.

S. J. Perelman (1904–1979)

485

What is true is what I can't help believing.

Oliver Wendell Holmes, Jr. (1841–1935)

486

I am the last of Britain's stately homos.

Quentin Crisp

487

I didn't want to be rich, I just wanted enough to get the couch reupholstered.

Kate (Mrs. Zero) Mostel

488

My father and he had one of those English friendships which begin by avoiding intimacies and eventually eliminate speech altogether.

Jorge Luis Borges

489

Shut up he explained.

Ring Lardner (1885–1933)

490
She had two complexions, A.M. and P.M.

Ring Lardner (1885–1933)

491
He writes so well he makes me feel like putting my quill back in my goose.

Fred Allen (1894–1956)

492
If my film makes one more person miserable, I'll feel I've done my job.

Woody Allen

493
The cloning of humans is on most of the lists of things to worry about from Science, along with behavior control, genetic engineering, transplanted heads, computer poetry and the unrestrained growth of plastic flowers.

Lewis Thomas

494
No one can earn a million dollars honestly.

William Jennings Bryan (1860–1925)

495
There are very few Japanese Jews. As a result, there is no Japanese word for Alan King.

Johnny Carson

496

From birth to age 18, a girl needs good parents, from 18 to 35 she needs good looks, from 35 to 55 she needs a good personality, and from 55 on she needs cash.

Sophie Tucker (1884?–1966)

497

Outer space is no place for a person of breeding.

Lady Violet Bonham Carter (1887–1969)

498

Our national flower is the concrete cloverleaf.

Lewis Mumford

499

The only normal people are the ones you don't know very well. *Joe Ancis*

500

You sofa-crevice fondler! *Peter De Vries*

501

Cats are like Baptists. They raise hell but you can't catch them at it. *Unknown*

502

So little time and so little to do.

Oscar Levant (1906–1972)

503

It's a rare person who wants to hear what he doesn't want to hear. *Dick Cavett*

504

When I hear the word "culture" I reach for my gun.

Hans Johst (c. 1939)

505

He washed his legs today and can't do a thing with them.

*Sportscaster Lon Simmons on seeing a baseball
player fall down twice in the first inning*

506

I like men to behave like men—strong and childish.

Françoise Sagan

507

A kleptomaniac is a person who helps himself because he can't help himself.   *Henry Morgan*

508

A hypocrite is a person who—but who isn't?

Don Marquis (1878–1937)

509

Brain damage reading test:

People tell me one thing and out the other. I feel as much like I did yesterday as I did today. I never liked room temperature. My throat is closer than it seems. Likes and dislikes are among my favorites. No napkin is sanitary enough for me. I don't like any of my loved ones.

Daniel M. Wegner

510

The two hardest things to handle in life are failure and success.   *Unknown*

511

Progress might have been all right once but it has gone on too long.   *Ogden Nash (1902–1971)*

512
I consider exercise vulgar. It makes people smell.
Alec Yuill Thornton

513
There is no human problem which could not be solved if people would simply do as I advise.
Gore Vidal

514
What's on your mind, if you will allow the overstatement?
Fred Allen (1894–1956)

515

The young man who has not wept is a savage, and the old man who will not laugh is a fool.

George Santayana (1866–1952)

516

Though I am not naturally honest, I am so sometimes by chance.   *Shakespeare (1564–1616)*

517

Early to rise and early to bed makes a male healthy, wealthy and dead.   *James Thurber (1894–1961)*

518

I have no relish for the country; it is a kind of healthy grave.

Sydney Smith (1771–1845)

519

A farm is an irregular patch of nettles, bound by short term notes, containing a fool and his wife who didn't know enough to stay in the city.

S. J. Perelman (1904–1979)

520

Everything has been figured out except how to live.

Jean-Paul Sartre (1905–1980)

521

Howard Hughes was able to afford the luxury of madness, like a man who not only thinks he is Napoleon but hires an army to prove it.   *Ted Morgan*

522

When it is not necessary to make a decision, it is necessary not to make a decision.

Lord Falkland (1610?–1643)

523

This book fills a much-needed gap.

Moses Hadas (1900–1966) in a review

524

Thank you for sending me a copy of your book. I'll waste no time reading it.

Moses Hadas (1900–1966) in a letter

525

There are plenty of good five-cent cigars in the country. The trouble is they cost a quarter. What this country really needs is a good five-cent nickel.

Franklin P. Adams (1881–1960)

526

Being perfectly well-dressed gives a feeling of tranquility that religion is powerless to bestow.

Ralph Waldo Emerson (1803–1882), quoting a friend

527

We are here and it is now. Further than that all human knowledge is moonshine.

H. L. Mencken (1880–1956)

528

There is no kind of dishonesty into which otherwise good people more easily and frequently fall than that of defrauding the government.

Benjamin Franklin (1706-1790)

529

Don't get the idea that I'm knocking the American system.

Al Capone (1899-1947)

530

It wasn't raining when Noah built the ark.

Howard Ruff

531

The learned are seldom pretty fellows, and in many cases their appearance tends to discourage a love of study in the young.

H. L. Mencken (1880-1956)

532

There is something going on now in Mexico that I happen to think is cruelty to animals. What I'm talking about, of course, is cat juggling.

Steve Martin

533

Truth is beautiful, without doubt; but so are lies.

Ralph Waldo Emerson (1803-1882)

534

We will march forward to a better tomorrow so long as separate groups like the blacks, the Negroes, and the coloreds can come together to work out their differences.

Steve Allen at a Redd Foxx roast

535

Ninety-eight percent of the adults in this country are decent, hard-working, honest Americans. It's the other lousy two percent that get all the publicity. But then—we elected them.

Lily Tomlin

536

There are more of them than us.

Herb Caen

537

Suppose you were an idiot and suppose you were a member of Congress. But I repeat myself.

Mark Twain (1835–1910)

538

Never go to bed mad. Stay up and fight.

Phyllis Diller

539

When I go to the beauty parlor, I always use the emergency entrance. Sometimes I just go for an estimate.

Phyllis Diller

540

Orthodox medicine has not found an answer to your complaint. However, luckily for you, I happen to be a quack.

Richter cartoon caption

541

One of a hostess's duties is to act as a procuress.

Marcel Proust (1871–1922)

542

Here is a supplementary bulletin from the Office of Fluctuation Control, Bureau of Edible Condiments, Soluble and Indigestible Fats and Glutinous Derivatives, Washington, D.C. Correction of Directive 943456201, issued a while back, concerning the fixed price of groundhog meat. In the directive above named, the quotation on groundhog meat should read ground hogmeat.

Bob and Ray

543

I've known what it is to be hungry, but I always went right to a restaurant. *Ring Lardner (1885–1933)*

544

What dreadful hot weather we have! It keeps me in a continual state of inelegance.

Jane Austen (1775–1817)

545

A single sentence will suffice for modern man: He fornicated and read the papers.

Albert Camus (1913–1960)

546

The rich are the scum of the earth in every country.

G. K. Chesterton (1874–1936)

547

One should never know too precisely whom one has married. *Nietzsche (1844–1900) on* Lohengrin

548

I never lecture, not because I am shy or a bad speaker, but simply because I detest the sort of people who go to lectures and don't want to meet them.

H. L. Mencken (1880–1956)

549

Bed is the poor man's opera.

Italian proverb

550

I'd rather be black than gay because when you're black you don't have to tell your mother.

Charles Pierce

551

Roses are red, violets are blue,
I'm a schizophrenic, and so am I.

Frank Crow

552

Lie Down and Roll Over and 159 Other Ways To Say I Love You.

1981 book title

553

I improve on misquotation.

Cary Grant

554

Partying is such sweet sorrow.

Jean Kerr

555

Honest criticism is hard to take, particularly from a relative, a friend, an acquaintance, or a stranger.

Franklin P. Jones

556

If any cleric or monk speaks jocular words, such as provoke laughter, let him be anathema.

Ordinance, Second Council of Constance (1418)

557

Better that a girl has beauty than brains because boys see better than they think.

Unknown

558

I talk to myself because I like dealing with a better class of people.

Jackie Mason

559

It is better to have a permanent income than to be fascinating.

Oscar Wilde (1854–1900)

560

I did not sleep. I never do when I am over-happy, over-unhappy, or in bed with a strange man.

Edna O'Brien

561

Dostoyevsky was one of those neurotics who recover their health and even their serenity when disaster at last occurs.

V. S. Pritchett

562

Exit, pursued by a bear.

Stage direction in Shakespeare's
The Winter's Tale *(1611)*

563

¿Como frijoles? (Spanish for How have you bean?)
Unknown

564

I don't make jokes. I just watch the government and report
the facts. *Will Rogers (1879–1935)*

565

Even in civilized mankind faint traces of monogamous instinct can be perceived.
Bertrand Russell (1872–1970)

566

Things to do in Burbank:
    1. Go to the Safeway parking lot for the roller skating festival called Holiday on Tar.

Johnny Carson

567

I would rather be a coward than brave because people hurt you when you are brave.

E. M. Forster (1879–1970) as a small child

568

One day there will be only five kings left, hearts, spades, diamonds, clubs, and England.

King Farouk (1920–1965) after his overthrow by Nasser

569

When ideas fail, words come in very handy.

Goethe (1749–1832)

570

Music with dinner is an insult both to the cook and the violinist.

G. K. Chesterton (1874–1936)

571

The place of the father in the modern suburban family is a very small one, particularly if he plays golf.

Bertrand Russell (1872–1970)

572

Avarice is the sphincter of the heart.

Matthew Green (c. 1737)

573

It is easier to be gigantic than to be beautiful.

Nietzsche (1844–1900)

574

By the time we've made it, we've had it.

Malcolm Forbes

575

I only like two kinds of men: domestic and foreign.

Mae West (1893–1980)

576

Where but in Kenya can a man whose grandfather was a cannibal watch a really good game of polo?

Marina Sulzberger (1920–1976)

577

France was a long despotism tempered by epigrams.

Thomas Carlyle (1795–1881)

578
Never trust anyone over-dirty.

Robert Byrne

579
There are more pleasant things to do than beat up people.
*Muhammad Ali on the occasion
of one of his retirements*

580
Mirrors and copulation are abominable because they in-
crease the numbers of men.

Jorge Luis Borges

581

I don't worry about getting old. I'm old already. Only young people worry about getting old. When I was 65 I had cupid's eczema. I don't believe in dying. It's been done. I'm working on a new exit. Besides, I can't die now—I'm booked.

George Burns

582

Men who never get carried away should be.

Malcolm Forbes

583

If you aren't fired with enthusiasm, you will be fired with enthusiasm. *Vince Lombardi (1913–1970)*

584

When I was kidnapped, my parents snapped into action. They rented out my room.

Woody Allen

585

The best cure for hypochondria is to forget about your body and get interested in somebody else's.

Goodman Ace (1899–1982)

586

New invention: Snap-on acne for people who want to look younger. *Johnny Carson*

587

Love teaches even asses to dance.

French proverb

588

Ammonia is beautiful.

Bumper sticker

589

FECK OPUC.

Bumper sticker

590

There is one fault that I must find
    With the twentieth century,
And I'll put it in a couple of words:
    Too adventury.
What I'd like would be some nice dull monotony
    If anyone's gotony.

Ogden Nash (1902–1971)

591

If called by a panther
Don't anther.

Ogden Nash (1902–1971)

592

First secure an independent income, then practice virtue.

Greek saying

593

What we call real estate—the solid ground to build a house
on—is the broad foundation on which nearly all of the guilt
of the world rests.

Nathaniel Hawthorne (1804–1864)

594

I have never liked working. To me a job is an invasion of
privacy.

Danny McGoorty (1901–1970)

595

Boy, the things I do for England.

Prince Charles on sampling snake meat

596

Victory goes to the player who makes the next-to-last mistake. *Savielly Grigorievitch Tartakower (1887–1956)*

597

Of all noises, I think music is the least disagreeable. *Samuel Johnson (1709–1784)*

598

One, two, three,
Buckle my shoe.

Robert Benchley (1889–1945)

599

It is rather to be chosen than great riches, unless I have
omitted something from the quotation.

Robert Benchley (1889–1945)
in Maxims From the Chinese

600

There must be 500,000 rats in the United States; of course,
I am only speaking from memory.

Billy Nye (1850–1896)

601

Newspapermen learn to call a murderer "an alleged murderer" and the King of England "the alleged King of England"
to avoid libel suits.

Stephen Leacock (1869–1944)

602

Lord Ronald said nothing; he flung himself from the room,
flung himself upon his horse and rode madly off in all direc-
tions.

Stephen Leacock (1869–1944)

603

I do not take a single newspaper, nor read one a month, and
I feel myself infinitely the happier for it.

Thomas Jefferson (1743–1826)

604

Show me a hero and I will write you a tragedy.

F. Scott Fitzgerald (1896–1940)

605

We can't all be heroes because somebody has to sit on the curb and clap as they go by.

Will Rogers (1879–1935)

606

Some things have to be believed to be seen.

Ralph Hodgson on ESP

607

One of the most astounding cases of clairvoyance is that of the noted Greek psychic Achilles Loudos. Loudos realized that he had unusual powers by the age of ten, when he could lie in bed and, by concentrating, make his father's false teeth jump out of his mouth.

Woody Allen

608

A cucumber should be well-sliced, dressed with pepper and vinegar, and then thrown out.

Samuel Johnson (1709–1784)

609

Middle age is when you've met so many people that every new person you meet reminds you of someone else.

Ogden Nash (1902–1971)

610

Wagner's music is better than it sounds.

Bill Nye (1850–1896)

611

With those delicate features of his he would have made a pretty woman, and he probably never has.

Josefa Heifetz

612
I don't want any yes-men around me. I want everybody to tell me the truth even if it costs them their jobs.

Samuel Goldwyn (1882–1974)

613
The advantage of the emotions is that they lead us astray.

Oscar Wilde (1854–1900)

614
In the first place, God made idiots. That was for practice. Then he made school boards.

Mark Twain (1835–1910)

615
She wears her clothes as if they were thrown on with a pitchfork.

Jonathan Swift (1667–1745)

616
A man is known by the company he avoids.

Unknown

617
Underneath this flabby exterior is an enormous lack of character.

Oscar Levant (1906–1972)

618
Nobody roots for Goliath.

Wilt Chamberlain

619

He went to Europe as a boy, where in Geneva his father arranged for a prostitute. He was so terrified by the experience that he didn't marry until he was 67 years old.

John Leonard on Borges

620

Keep breathing.

Sophie Tucker (1884?–1966)

621

If people don't want to come out to the ball park, nobody's going to stop them.   *Yogi Berra*

622

Tradition is what you resort to when you don't have the time or the money to do it right.

Kurt Herbert Adler (1905–1988)

623

It is impossible to imagine Goethe or Beethoven being good at billiards or golf.

H. L. Mencken (1880–1956)

624

All truths are half-truths.

Alfred North Whitehead (1861–1947)

625

To generalize is to be an idiot.

William Blake (1757–1827)

626

If you look like your passport photo, you're too ill to travel.

Will Kommen

627

How can one conceive of a one-party system in a country that has over 200 varieties of cheese?

Charles de Gaulle (1890–1970)

628

When you have got an elephant by the hind legs and he is trying to run away, it is best to let him run.

Abraham Lincoln (1809–1865)

629

After three days, fish and guests stink.

John Lyly (1554?–1606)

630

I was born in Australia because my mother wanted me to be near her. *Unknown*

631

I will always cherish the initial misconceptions I had about you. *Unknown*

632

The majority of those who put together collections of verses or epigrams resemble those who eat cherries or oysters; they begin by choosing the best and end by eating everything. *Chamfort (1741–1794)*

633

If you were a member of Jesse James's band and people asked you what you were, you wouldn't say, "Well, I'm a desperado." You'd say something like, "I work in banks," or "I've done some railroad work." It took me a long time just to say "I'm a writer." It's really embarrassing.

Roy Blount, Jr.

634

It takes about ten years to get used to how old you are.

Unknown

635

After all is said and done, more is said than done.

Unknown

636

In the end, everything is a gag.

Charlie Chaplin (1889–1977)

637

Science has not yet found a cure for the pun.

Robert Byrne

The Other
637 Best Things
Anybody Ever Said

To
Tom Stewart,
who has kept so much egg off my face

Part I

Theology, Self-love, Self-abuse, Love, Sex, Wedlock, Kids, Drink, Death, Comedy, Men and Women, War, Money, Work and a great deal more

1

My theology, briefly, is that the universe was dictated but not signed.   *Christopher Morley (1890–1957)*

2

God made everything out of nothing, but the nothingness shows through.   *Paul Valéry (1871–1945)*

3

God was satisfied with his own work, and that is fatal.
                    Samuel Butler (1835–1902)

4

God is not dead but alive and well and working on a much less ambitious project.   *Graffito*

5

Why attack God? He may be as miserable as we are.
                    Erik Satie (1866–1925)

6

Every day people are straying away from the church and going back to God.

                    Lenny Bruce (1923–1966)

7

Religion is what keeps the poor from murdering the rich.
                    Napoleon (1769–1821)

8

What if there had been room at the inn?
Linda Festa on the origins of Christianity

9

Christ died for our sins. Dare we make his martyrdom meaningless by not committing them?

Jules Feiffer

10

Catholicism has changed tremendously in recent years. Now when Communion is served there is also a salad bar.

Bill Maher

11

Faith is believing what you know ain't so.
"A schoolboy" quoted by Mark Twain (1835–1910)

12

Faith is under the left nipple.

Martin Luther (1483–1546)

13

Because I'm Jewish, a lot of people ask why I killed Christ. What can I say? It was an accident. It was one of those parties that got out of hand. I killed him because he wouldn't become a doctor.   *Lenny Bruce (1923–1966)*

14

Your chances of getting hit by lightning go up if you stand under a tree, shake your fist at the sky, and say, "Storms suck!" *Johnny Carson*

15

Trust in Allah, but tie your camel.

Arabian proverb

16

The last time I saw him he was walking down Lover's Lane holding his own hand.

Fred Allen (1894–1956)

17

The nice thing about egotists is that they don't talk about other people. *Lucille S. Harper*

18

It is far more impressive when others discover your good qualities without your help.

Miss Manners (Judith Martin)

19

In an age when the fashion is to be in love with yourself, confessing to be in love with somebody else is an admission of unfaithfulness to one's beloved.

Russell Baker

20

If only it was as easy to banish hunger by rubbing the belly as it is to masturbate.

Diogenes the Cynic (412? to 323 B.C.)

21

Self-abuse is the most certain road to the grave.

Dr. George M. Calhoun in 1855

22

Many mothers are wholly ignorant of the almost universal prevalence of secret vice, or self-abuse, among the young. Why hesitate to say firmly and without quibble that personal abuse lies at the root of much of the feebleness, paleness, nervousness, and good-for-nothingness of the entire community? *Dr. J. H. Kellogg (1852–1943)*

23

Masturbation! The amazing availability of it!

James Joyce (1882–1941)

24

Philosophy is to the real world as masturbation is to sex.

Karl Marx (1818–1883)

25

I was the best I ever had.

Woody Allen

26

The good thing about masturbation is that you don't have to dress up for it.

Truman Capote (1924–1984)

27

My brain is my second favorite organ.

Woody Allen

28

Love is not the dying moan of a distant violin—it's the triumphant twang of a bedspring.

S. J. Perelman (1904–1979)

29

Love is what you've been through with somebody.

James Thurber (1894–1961)

30

Love is the delusion that one woman differs from another.

H. L. Mencken (1880–1956)

31

Love is being stupid together.

Paul Valéry (1871–1945)

32

Love is an obsessive delusion that is cured by marriage.

Dr. Karl Bowman (1888–1973)

33

Love is the only game that is not called on account of darkness.

M. Hirschfield

34

The greatest love is a mother's, then a dog's, then a sweetheart's.

Polish proverb

35

If I love you, what business is it of yours?

Johann von Goethe (1749–1832)

36

A man in love mistakes a pimple for a dimple.

Japanese proverb

37

A lover without indiscretion is no lover at all.

Thomas Hardy (1840–1928)

38

The most important thing in a relationship between a man and a woman is that one of them be good at taking orders.

Linda Festa

39

In a great romance, each person basically plays a part that the other really likes.

Elizabeth Ashley

40

I love Mickey Mouse more than any woman I've ever known.

Walt Disney (1901–1966)

41

I like young girls. Their stories are shorter.

Tom McGuane

42

The most romantic thing any woman ever said to me in bed was "Are you sure you're not a cop?"

Larry Brown

43

Someday we'll look back on this moment and plow into a parked car.

Evan Davis

44

Sex is dirty only when it's done right.

Unknown

45

For flavor, instant sex will never supersede the stuff you have to peel and cook.

Quentin Crisp

46

Why won't you let me kiss you goodnight? Is it something I said?

Tom Ryan

47

Give a man a free hand and he'll run it all over you.

Mae West (1892–1980)

48

I've been in more laps than a napkin.

Mae West (1892–1980)

49

I used to be Snow White, but I drifted.

Mae West (1892–1980)

50

He who hesitates is a damned fool.

Mae West (1892–1980)

51

I wasn't kissing her, I was whispering in her mouth.

Chico Marx (1891–1961)

52

Contraceptives should be used on every conceivable occasion.   *From* The Last Goon Show of All

53

Bisexuality immediately doubles your chances for a date on Saturday night.   *Woody Allen*

54

What do hookers do on their nights off, type?

Elayne Boosler

55

I have perfumed my bed with myrrh, aloes, and cinnamon.
Come, let us take our fill of love until the morning.

Proverbs 7:17–18

56

All the men on my staff can type.

Bella Abzug

57

A is for Apple.   *Hester Prynne*

58

The perfect lover is one who turns into a pizza at 4:00 A.M.
                                                Charles Pierce

59

If God had meant us to have group sex, he'd have given us
more organs.   *Malcolm Bradbury*

60

It's been so long since I made love I can't even remember
who gets tied up.   *Joan Rivers*

61

Ouch! That felt good!   *Karen Elizabeth Gordon*

62

I never expected to see the day when girls would get sun-
burned in the places they do today.

                              Will Rogers (1879–1935)

63

The first time we slept together she drove a recreational vehicle into the bedroom.

Richard Lewis

64

A man can sleep around, no questions asked, but if a woman makes nineteen or twenty mistakes she's a tramp.

Joan Rivers

65

What do you give a man who has everything? Penicillin.

Jerry Lester

66

Some men are so macho they'll get you pregnant just to kill a rabbit.

Maureen Murphy

67

Chaste makes waste.

Unknown

68

The trouble with incest is that it gets you involved with relatives.

George S. Kaufman (1889–1961)

69

After we made love he took a piece of chalk and made an outline of my body.   *Joan Rivers*

70

It's easy to make a friend. What's hard is to make a stranger.   *Unknown*

71

The reason people sweat is so they won't catch fire when making love.   *Don Rose*

72

Hc's such a hick he doesn't even have a trapeze in his bedroom.   *Unknown*

73

I'm against group sex because I wouldn't know where to put my elbows.   *Martin Cruz Smith*

74

If you want to read about love and marriage you've got to buy two separate books.

Alan King

75

'Tis more blessed to give than receive; for example, wedding presents.   *H. L. Mencken (1880–1956)*

76

Men have a much better time of it than women; for one thing they marry later; for another thing they die earlier.

H. L. Mencken (1880–1956)

77

Monogamy is the Western custom of one wife and hardly any mistresses.

H. H. Munro (Saki) (1870–1916)

78

Marriage is based on the theory that when a man discovers a brand of beer exactly to his taste he should at once throw up his job and go to work in the brewery.

George Jean Nathan (1882–1958)

79

A wife lasts only for the length of the marriage, but an ex-wife is there *for the rest of your life.*

Jim Samuels

80

A man in love is incomplete until he is married. Then he is finished.

Zsa Zsa Gabor

81

A husband is what is left of the lover after the nerve has been extracted.

Helen Rowland (1876–1950)

82

When a girl marries she exchanges the attentions of many men for the inattention of one.

Helen Rowland (1876–1950)

83

One man's folly is another man's wife.

Helen Rowland (1876–1950)

84

The most happy marriage I can imagine to myself would be the union of a deaf man to a blind woman.

Samuel Taylor Coleridge (1772–1834)

85

The trouble with some women is that they get all excited about nothing—and then marry him.

Cher

86

Trust your husband, adore your husband, and get as much as you can in your own name.

Advice to Joan Rivers from her mother

87

Honesty has ruined more marriages than infidelity.

Charles McCabe (1915–1983)

88

Bachelors should be heavily taxed. It is not fair that some men should be happier than others.

Oscar Wilde (1854–1900)

89

I believe in the institution of marriage and I intend to keep trying until I get it right. *Richard Pryor*

90

I was a fifty-four-year-old virgin, but I'm all right now.

Unknown

91

Eighty percent of married men cheat in America. The rest cheat in Europe.   *Jackie Mason*

92

A man can have two, maybe three love affairs while he's married. After that it's cheating.

Yves Montand

93

Marriage has driven more than one man to sex.

Peter De Vries

94

It destroys one's nerves to be amiable every day to the same human being.

Benjamin Disraeli (1804–1881)

95

If you are looking for a kindly, well-to-do older gentleman who is no longer interested in sex, take out an ad in *The Wall Street Journal.*   *Abigail Van Buren*

96

Divorce is a game played by lawyers.

Cary Grant

97

She cried, and the judge wiped her tears with my checkbook.

Tommy Manville (1894–1967)

98

I can't mate in captivity.   *Gloria Steinem on why she has never married*

99

It wasn't exactly a divorce—I was traded.

Tim Conway

100

You don't know anything about a woman until you meet her in court.   *Norman Mailer*

101

I'm very old-fashioned. I believe that people should marry for life, like pigeons and Catholics.

Woody Allen

102

Marriage is like a bank account. You put it in, you take it out, you lose interest.   *Professor Irwin Corey*

103

I hate babies. They're so human.

H. H. Munro (Saki) (1870–1916)

104

The baby was so ugly they had to hang a pork chop around its neck to get the dog to play with it.

Unknown

105

My mother didn't breast-feed me. She said she liked me as a friend.

Rodney Dangerfield

106

It is no wonder that people are so horrible when they start life as children.

Kingsley Amis

107

I was toilet-trained at gunpoint.

Billy Braver

108

Life does not begin at the moment of conception or the moment of birth. It begins when the kids leave home and the dog dies.   *Unknown*

109

One father is more than a hundred schoolmasters.
                              George Herbert (1593–1633)

110

An ounce of mother is worth a ton of priest.
                                              Spanish proverb

111

Happy is the child whose father died rich.

                                                      Proverb

112

Reinhart was never his mother's favorite—and he was an only child.   *Thomas Berger*

113

Nature makes boys and girls lovely to look upon so they can be tolerated until they acquire some sense.
                              William Lyon Phelps (1865–1943)

114

The first half of our lives is ruined by our parents and the second half by our children.

Clarence Darrow (1857–1938)

115

Literature is mostly about having sex and not much about having children. Life is the other way around.

David Lodge

116

If you have never been hated by your child, you have never been a parent.

Bette Davis

117

How to Raise Your I.Q. by Eating Gifted Children

Book title by Lewis B. Frumkes (1983)

118

Never raise your hand to your children—it leaves your midsection unprotected.

Robert Orben

119

Blessed are the young, for they shall inherit the national debt.

Herbert Hoover (1874–1964)

120

The denunciation of the young is a necessary part of the hygiene of older people, and greatly assists in the circulation of the blood.

Logan Pearsall Smith (1865–1946)

121

One of the disadvantages of having children is that they eventually get old enough to give you presents they make at school. *Robert Byrne*

122

Never have children, only grandchildren.

Gore Vidal

123

No matter how old a mother is, she watches her middle-aged children for signs of improvement.

Florida Scott-Maxwell

124

Youth is such a wonderful thing. What a crime to waste it on children. *George Bernard Shaw (1856–1950)*

125

Having children is like having a bowling alley installed in your brain. *Martin Mull*

126

If you think education is expensive, try ignorance.

Derek Bok

127

I'm for bringing back the birch, but only for consenting adults.
Gore Vidal

128

Education is the process of casting false pearls before real swine.
Irwin Edman (1896–1954)

129

Good teaching is one-fourth preparation and three-fourths theatre.
Gail Godwin

130

University politics are vicious precisely because the stakes are so small.
Henry Kissinger

131

Political history is far too criminal a subject to be a fit thing to teach children. *W. H. Auden (1907–1973)*

132

I think the world is run by C students.

Al McGuire

133

Smartness runs in my family. When I went to school I was so smart my teacher was in my class for five years.

George Burns

134

You can't expect a boy to be vicious till he's been to a good school. *H. H. Munro (Saki) (1870–1916)*

135

I was thrown out of college for cheating on the metaphysics exam; I looked into the soul of the boy next to me.

Woody Allen

136

Beware of the man who does not drink.

Proverb

137

Water, taken in moderation, cannot hurt anybody.

Mark Twain (1835–1910)

138

A productive drunk is the bane of moralists.

Unknown

139

Come quickly, I am tasting stars!

Dom Pérignon (1638–1715) at the moment of his discovery of champagne

140

The worst thing about some men is that when they are not drunk they are sober.

William Butler Yeats (1865–1939)

141

An Irishman is not drunk as long as he still has a blade of grass to hang onto.

Unknown

142

Alcohol is the anesthesia by which we endure the operation of life. *George Bernard Shaw (1856–1950)*

143

To drink is a Christian diversion, unknown to the Turk or the Persian. *William Congreve (1670–1729)*

144

To one large turkey add one gallon of vermouth and a demi-john of Angostura bitters. Shake.

Recipe for turkey cocktail from F. Scott Fitzgerald
(1896–1940)

145

An alcoholic is someone you don't like who drinks as much as you do. *Dylan Thomas (1914–1953)*

146

I can't die until the government finds a safe place to bury my liver. *Phil Harris*

147

My uncle was the town drunk—and we lived in Chicago.
George Gobel

148

I've never been drunk, but often I've been overserved.
George Gobel

149

Somebody left the cork out of my lunch.
W. C. Fields (1880–1946)

150

I have to think hard to name an interesting man who does not drink. *Richard Burton*

151

I always wake up at the crack of ice.

Joe E. Lewis (1902–1971)

152

The graveyards are full of indispensable men.

Charles de Gaulle (1890–1970)

153

There are more dead people than living, and their numbers are increasing.

Eugène Ionesco

154
Defeat is worse than death because you have to live with
defeat.
                                                    Bill Musselman

155

The executioner is, I hear, very expert, and my neck is very slender.   *Anne Boleyn (1507?–1536)*

156

I didn't know he was dead; I thought he was British.

Unknown

157

I believe in sex and death—two experiences that come once in a lifetime.   *Woody Allen*

158

There are worse things in life than death. Have you ever spent an evening with an insurance salesman?

Woody Allen

159

Go away. I'm all right.   *Last words of H. G. Wells*
(1885–1946)

160

You can pretend to be serious; you can't pretend to be witty.

Sacha Guitry (1885–1957)

161

Everybody likes a kidder, but nobody lends him money.

Arthur Miller

162

One doesn't have a sense of humor. It has you.

Larry Gelbart

163

The aim of a joke is not to degrade the human being but to remind him that he is already degraded.

George Orwell (1903–1950)

164

If you don't count some of Jehovah's injunctions, there are no humorists in the Bible.

Mordecai Richler

165

Dying is easy. Comedy is difficult.

Actor Edmund Gwenn (1875–1959) on his deathbed

166

Humorists always sit at the children's table.

Woody Allen

167

I don't care where I sit as long as I get fed.

Calvin Trillin

168

What is comedy? Comedy is the art of making people laugh without making them puke.

Steve Martin

169

Until Eve arrived, this was a man's world.

Richard Armour

170

Whatever women do they must do twice as well as men to be thought half as good. Luckily, this is not difficult.

Charlotte Whitton (1896–1975)

171

Don't accept rides from strange men, and remember that all men are strange.

Robin Morgan

172
There are only two kinds of men—the dead and the deadly.
Helen Rowland (1876–1950)

173
Men are creatures with two legs and eight hands.
Jayne Mansfield (1932–1967)

174
I refuse to consign the whole male sex to the nursery. I insist on believing that some men are my equals.
Brigid Brophy

175
Being a woman is a terribly difficult trade, since it consists principally of dealing with men.
Joseph Conrad (1857–1924)

176
Being a woman is of special interest to aspiring male transexuals. To actual women it is simply a good excuse not to play football.
Fran Lebowitz

177
My advice to the women's clubs of America is to raise more hell and fewer dahlias.
William Allen White (1868–1944)

178
A lady is one who never shows her underwear uninten-
tionally.   *Lillian Day*

179
Anyone who says he can see through women is missing a lot.
Groucho Marx (1895–1977)

180
The most popular labor-saving device today is still a husband with money.   *Joey Adams*

181
A gentleman never strikes a lady with his hat on.
Fred Allen (1894–1956)

182
I've never struck a woman in my life, not even my own
mother.   *W. C. Fields (1880–1946)*

183
If you become a star, *you* don't change, everyone else does.
Kirk Douglas

184
I'm not a real movie star—I've still got the same wife I started
out with twenty-eight years ago.
Will Rogers (1879–1935)

185
Fame lost its appeal for me when I went into a public restroom and an autograph seeker handed me a pen and paper under the stall door. *Marlo Thomas*

186
If I had done everything I'm credited with, I'd be speaking to you from a laboratory jar at Harvard.

Frank Sinatra

187
AS USUAL, YOUR INFORMATION STINKS.
Telegram to Time *magazine from Frank Sinatra*

188
As an anti-American, I thank you for your rotten article devoted to my person. *Letter to* Time *magazine from Prince Sihanouk*

189
I am a deeply superficial person.

Andy Warhol

190
I have bursts of being a lady, but it doesn't last long.
Shelley Winters

191

Working with Julie Andrews is like getting hit over the head with a valentine.   *Christopher Plummer*

192

I should have been a country-western singer. After all, I'm older than most western countries.

George Burns

193

Never face facts; if you do you'll never get up in the morning.

Marlo Thomas

194

Nothing succeeds like the appearance of success.

Christopher Lascl

195

She's the kind of girl who climbed the ladder of success wrong by wrong.

Mae West (1892–1980)

196

Nothing fails like success.

Gerald Nachman

197

Anyone seen on a bus after the age of thirty has been a failure in life.

Loelia, Duchess of Westminster

198

To err is human
And stupid.   *Robert Byrne*

199

You may already be a loser.
Form letter received by Rodney Dangerfield

200

How should they answer?
*Abigail Van Buren in reply to the question
"Why do Jews always answer a question with a
question?"*

201

If you live in New York, even if you're Catholic, you're Jewish.   *Lenny Bruce (1923–1966)*

202

Jews always know two things: suffering and where to find great Chinese food.

From the movie My Favorite Year, *1982*

203

The goys have proven the following theorem. . . .

Physicist John von Neumann (1903–1957)
at the start of a classroom lecture

204

I want to be the white man's brother, not his brother-in-law.

Martin Luther King, Jr. (1929–1968)

205

I have just enough white in me to make my honesty questionable.

Will Rogers (1879–1935)

206

I never believed in Santa Claus because I knew no white dude would come into my neighborhood after dark.

Dick Gregory

207

Work is of two kinds: first, altering the position of matter at or near the earth's surface relative to other matter; second, telling other people to do so.

Bertrand Russell (1872–1970)

208

All jobs should be open to everybody, unless they actually require a penis or vagina.

Florynce Kennedy

209

It is impossible to enjoy idling unless there is plenty of work to do.   *Jerome K. Jerome (1859–1927)*

210

Anybody who works is a fool. I don't work, I merely inflict myself on the public.　　　　　　　　　*Robert Morley*

211

Hard work never killed anybody, but why take a chance?
　　　　　　Charlie McCarthy (Edgar Bergen, 1903–1978)

212

If you have a job without aggravations, you don't have a job.
　　　　　　　　　　　　　　　　Malcolm Forbes

213

People who work sitting down get paid more than people who work standing up.

　　　　　　　　　　　　Ogden Nash (1902–1971)

214

Work is much more fun than fun.
　　　　　　　　　　　Noel Coward (1899–1973)

215

The trouble with the rat race is that even if you win you're still a rat.　　　　　　　　　　　　*Lily Tomlin*

216

Money is good for bribing yourself through the inconveniences of life.　　　　　　　　*Gottfried Reinhardt*

217

A billion here, a billion there—pretty soon it adds up to real money.   *Senator Everett Dirksen (1896–1969)*

218

I have enough money to last me the rest of my life, unless I buy something.   *Jackie Mason*

219

The rich have a passion for bargains as lively as it is pointless.   *Françoise Sagan*

220

Whoever said money can't buy happiness didn't know where to shop.   *Unknown*

221

Behind every great fortune there is a crime.
Honoré de Balzac (1799–1850)

222

The richer your friends, the more they will cost you.
Elisabeth Marbury (1856–1933)

223

Money is always there, but the pockets change.
Gertrude Stein (1874–1946)

224

There must be more to life than having everything.

Maurice Sendak

225

If women didn't exist, all the money in the world would have no meaning. *Aristotle Onassis (1906–1975)*

226

Better to be nouveau than never to have been riche at all.

Unknown

227

Save a little money each month and at the end of the year you'll be surprised at how little you have.

Ernest Haskins

228

My problem lies in reconciling my gross habits with my net income. *Errol Flynn (1909–1959)*

229

Any man who has $10,000 left when he dies is a failure.

Errol Flynn (1909–1959)

230

The wages of sin are unreported.

Unknown

231

I'm living so far beyond my income that we may almost be said to be living apart.

e e cummings (1894–1962)

232

To get back on your feet, miss two car payments.

Unknown

233

When I first arrived in this country I had only fifteen cents in my pocket and a willingness to compromise.

Weber cartoon caption

234

Fashion is a form of ugliness so intolerable that we have to alter it every six months.   *Oscar Wilde (1856–1900)*

235

If you look good and dress well, you don't need a purpose in life.   *Fashion consultant Robert Pante*

236

Every generation laughs at the old fashions but religiously follows the new.

Henry David Thoreau (1817–1862)

237

I base my fashion taste on what doesn't itch.

Gilda Radner

238

War is a series of catastrophes that results in a victory.

Georges Clemenceau (1841–1929)

239

You can no more win a war than you can win an earthquake.

Jeannette Rankin (1880–1973)

240

I'd like to see the government get out of war altogether and leave the whole field to private industry.

Joseph Heller

241

The object of war is not to die for your country but to make the other bastard die for his.

General George Patton (1885–1945)

242

Name me an emperor who was ever struck by a cannonball.

Charles V (1500–1558)

243

While you're saving your face you're losing your ass.

President Lyndon Johnson (1908–1973)

244

You can't say civilization don't advance . . . in every war they kill you a new way.

Will Rogers (1879–1935)

245

I have already given two cousins to the war and I stand ready to sacrifice my wife's brother.

Artemus Ward (1834–1867)

246

Join the army, see the world, meet interesting people, and
kill them. *Unknown*

247

Being in the army is like being in the Boy Scouts, except that
the Boy Scouts have adult supervision.

Blake Clark

248

The Israelis are the Doberman pinschers of the Middle East.
They treat the Arabs like postmen.

Franklyn Ajaye

Part II

Advice, Health, Food, Life Itself, America, Psychoses, Books, Writers, Music, Show Business, Animals, Doctors, Presidents, Politics, Sports and much else

249

Start slow and taper off.

Walt Stack

250

Never get into fights with ugly people because they have nothing to lose.

Unknown

251

Never miss a good chance to shut up.

Scott Beach's grandfather

252

The best way to keep one's word is not to give it.

Napoleon (1769–1821)

253

It's all right letting yourself go as long as you can let yourself back.

Mick Jagger

254

Sometimes a scream is better than a thesis.

Ralph Waldo Emerson (1803–1882)

255

Aaeeeyaaayaaayaayaa . . .

Johnny Weissmuller (1904–1984)

256

When walking through a melon patch, don't adjust your sandals.
Chinese proverb

257

Sometimes a fool makes a good suggestion.
Nicolas Boileau (1636–1711)

258

Good advice is one of those insults that ought to be forgiven.
Unknown

259

It's no longer a question of staying healthy. It's a question of finding a sickness you like.
Jackie Mason

260

I've just learned about his illness. Let's hope it's nothing trivial.
Variously ascribed

261

I don't deserve this award, but I have arthritis and I don't deserve that either.
Jack Benny (1894–1974)

262

As for me, except for an occasional heart attack, I feel as young as I ever did.
Robert Benchley (1889–1945)

263

I get my exercise acting as a pallbearer to my friends who exercise.
Chauncey Depew (1834–1928)

264

Avoid running at all time.
Satchel Paige (1906?–1982)

265

It is more profitable for your congressman to support the tobacco industry than your life.
Jackie Mason

266

Smoking is one of the leading causes of statistics.
Fletcher Knebel

267

Quit worrying about your health. It'll go away.
Robert Orben

268

Health nuts are going to feel stupid someday, lying in hospitals dying of nothing.
Redd Foxx

269

To eat is human
To digest divine.
Mark Twain (1835–1910)

270

There is no sincerer love than the love of food.
George Bernard Shaw (1856–1950)

271

The most dangerous food is wedding cake.

American proverb

272

Roumanian-Yiddish cooking has killed more Jews than Hitler.

Zero Mostel (1915–1977)

273

I believe that eating pork makes people stupid.

David Steinberg

274

Eat, drink, and be merry, for tomorrow we may diet.

Unknown

275

When men reach their sixties and retire, they go to pieces. Women go right on cooking.

Gail Sheehy

276
I've been on a diet for two weeks and all I've lost is two
weeks. *Totie Fields (1931–1978)*

277
I'm on a seafood diet. I see food and I eat it.
Variously ascribed

278
Eat as much as you like—just don't swallow it.
Steve Burns

279
Put a pot of chili on the stove to simmer.
Let it simmer. Meanwhile, broil a good steak.
Eat the steak. Let the chili simmer. Ignore it.
*Recipe for chili from Allan Shivers,
former governor of Texas*

280
The two biggest sellers in any bookstore are the cookbooks
and the diet books. The cookbooks tell you how to prepare
the food and the diet books tell you how not to eat any
of it. *Andy Rooney*

281
It's so beautifully arranged on the plate—you know some-
one's fingers have been all over it.
Julia Child on nouvelle cuisine

282

A gourmet who thinks of calories is like a tart who looks at her watch.
James Beard

283

Where do you go to get anorexia?

Shelley Winters

284

Nachman's Rule: When it comes to foreign food, the less authentic the better.

Gerald Nachman

285

I eat merely to put food out of my mind.

N. F. Simpson

286

Isn't there any other part of the matzo you can eat?
*Marilyn Monroe (1926–1962) on being served
matzo ball soup three meals in a row*

287

A gourmet restaurant in Cincinnati is one where you leave the tray on the table after you eat.

Unknown

288

When compelled to cook, I produce a meal that would make a sword swallower gag. *Russell Baker*

289

Poets have been mysteriously silent on the subject of cheese. *G. K. Chesterton (1874–1936)*

290

I don't even butter my bread. I consider that cooking. *Katherine Cebrian*

291

Life is too short to stuff a mushroom.

Storm Jameson

292

The most remarkable thing about my mother is that for thirty years she served the family nothing but leftovers. The original meal has never been found.

Calvin Trillin

293

I'm in favor of liberalized immigration because of the effect it would have on restaurants. I'd let just about everybody in except the English.   *Calvin Trillin*

294

No man is lonely while eating spaghetti.

Robert Morley

295

I prefer my oysters fried;
That way I know my oysters died.

Roy G. Blount, Jr.

296

The trouble with life in the fast lane is that you get to the other end in an awful hurry.

John Jensen

297

It is not true that life is one damn thing after another—it is one damn thing over and over.

Edna St. Vincent Millay (1892–1950)

298

Life is thirst.

Leonard Michaels

299

The less things change, the more they remain the same.

Sicilian proverb

300

There are days when it takes all you've got just to keep up with the losers. *Robert Orben*

301

If you can see the light at the end of the tunnel you are looking the wrong way.

Barry Commoner

302

I have found little that is good about human beings. In my experience most of them are trash.

Sigmund Freud (1856–1939)

303

The brotherhood of man is not a mere poet's dream; it is a most depressing and humiliating reality.

Oscar Wilde (1854–1900)

304

We're all in this alone. *Lily Tomlin*

305

Our ignorance of history makes us libel our own times. People have always been like this.

Gustave Flaubert (1821–1880)

306

The British tourist is always happy abroad so long as the natives are waiters. *Robert Morley*

307

You can't judge Egypt by *Aïda.*

Ronald Firbank

308

France is a country where the money falls apart and you can't tear the toilet paper.

Billy Wilder

309

In Marseilles they make half the toilet soap we consume in America, but the Marseillaise only have a vague theoretical idea of its use, which they have obtained from books of travel. *Mark Twain (1835–1910)*

310

Gaiety is the most outstanding feature of the Soviet Union.
Joseph Stalin (1879–1953)

311

In Italy, for thirty years under the Borgias, they had warfare,
terror, murder, and bloodshed, but they produced Michelan-
gelo, Leonardo da Vinci, and the Renaissance. In Switzer-
land, they had brotherly love, they had five hundred years
of democracy and peace—and what did they produce? The
cuckoo clock.

From the movie The Third Man, *1949*

312

Canada is so square even the female impersonators are
women. *From the movie* Outrageous, *1983*

313

Most Texans think Hanukkah is some sort of duck call.

Richard Lewis

314

Historians have now definitely established that Juan Cabrillo,
discoverer of California, was not looking for Kansas, thus
setting a precedent that continues to this day.

Wayne Shannon

315

The big cities of America are becoming Third World countries. *Nora Ephron*

316
New York now leads the world's great cities in the number of people around whom you shouldn't make a sudden move.
David Letterman

317
It isn't necessary to have relatives in Kansas City in order to be unhappy. *Groucho Marx (1895–1977)*

318
Isn't it nice that people who prefer Los Angeles to San Francisco live there? *Herb Caen*

319
San Francisco is like granola: Take away the fruits and the nuts, and all you have are the flakes.
Unknown

320
In San Francisco, Halloween is redundant.
Will Durst

321
Detroit is Cleveland without the glitter.
Unknown

322

When I saw a sign on the freeway that said, "Los Angeles 445 miles," I said to myself, "I've got to get out of this lane."

Franklyn Ajaye

323

Traffic signals in New York are just rough guidelines.

David Letterman

324

I have an existential map. It has "You are here" written all over it.   *Steven Wright*

325

I hate small towns because once you've seen the cannon in the park there's nothing else to do.
                              Lenny Bruce (1923–1966)

326

Schizophrenia beats dining alone.
                              Unknown

327

When we talk to God, we're praying. When God talks to us, we're schizophrenic.   *Lily Tomlin*

328

When dealing with the insane, the best method is to pretend to be sane.   *Hermann Hesse (1877–1962)*

329

I don't really trust a sane person.
                              Pro football lineman Lyle Alzado

330

Sometimes when you look in his eyes you get the feeling that someone else is driving.
                              David Letterman

331

I'm going to give my psychoanalyst one more year, then I'm going to Lourdes. *Woody Allen*

332

When a book and a head collide and there is a hollow sound, is it always from the book?

Georg Christoph Lichtenberg (1742–1799)

333

I've given up reading books. I find it takes my mind off myself. *Oscar Levant (1906–1972)*

334

Where do I find the time for not reading so many books?

Karl Kraus (1874–1936)

335

A person who publishes a book appears willfully in public with his pants down.

Edna St. Vincent Millay (1892–1950)

336

The reason why so few good books are written is that so few people who can write know anything.

Walter Bagehot (1826–1877)

337

The newspaper is the natural enemy of the book, as the whore is of the decent woman.

The Goncourt Brothers, 1858

338

Manuscript: Something submitted in haste and returned at leisure.

Oliver Herford (1863–1935)

339

Your manuscript is both good and original, but the part that is good is not original and the part that is original is not good.

Samuel Johnson (1709–1784)

340

Autobiography is an unrivaled vehicle for telling the truth about other people.

Philip Guedalla (1889–1944)

341

A well-written life is almost as rare as a well-spent one.

Thomas Carlyle (1795–1881)

342

I have read your book and much like it.

Moses Hadas (1900–1966)

343

A novel is a piece of prose of a certain length with something wrong with it.

Unknown

344

There are two kinds of books: those that no one reads and those that no one ought to read.

H. L. Mencken (1880–1956)

345

The covers of this book are too far apart.

Ambrose Bierce (1842–1914?)

346

[He] took me into his library and showed me his books, of which he had a complete set.

Ring Lardner (1885–1933)

347

The man who reads nothing at all is better educated than the man who reads nothing but newspapers.

Thomas Jefferson (1743–1826)

348

Journalism largely consists in saying "Lord Jones is dead" to people who never knew Lord Jones was alive.

G. K. Chesterton (1874–1936)

349

There is so much to be said in favor of modern journalism. By giving us the opinions of the uneducated it keeps us in touch with ignorance of the community.

Oscar Wilde (1854–1900)

350

Small Earthquake in Chile;
Not Many Killed

Headline suggested for
The Times *of London by Claud Cockburn*

351

Writers have two main problems. One is writer's block, when the words won't come at all, and the other is logorrhea, when the words come so fast that they can hardly get to the wastebasket in time.

Cecilia Bartholomew

352

All of us learn to write in the second grade. Most of us go on to greater things.

Basketball coach Bobby Knight

353

When writers refer to themselves as "we" and to the reader as "you," it's two against one.

Judith Rascoe

354

Most writers regard the truth as their most valuable possession, and therefore are most economical in its use.

Mark Twain (1835–1910)

355

Writing is turning one's worst moments into money.

J. P. Donleavy

356

Writing is the only profession in which one can make no money without being ridiculous.

Jules Renard (1864–1910)

357

Writers should be read, but neither seen nor heard.

Daphne Du Maurier

358

If you can't annoy somebody, there is little point in writing.

Kingsley Amis

359

Unprovided with original learning, unformed in the habits of thinking, unskilled in the arts of composition, I resolved to write a book.   *Edward Gibbon (1737–1794)*

360

Everywhere I go I'm asked if I think the university stifles writers. My opinion is that they don't stifle enough of them. There's many a bestseller that could have been prevented by a good teacher.

Flannery O'Connor (1925–1964)

361

Great Moments in Literature: In 1936, Ernest Hemingway, while trout fishing, caught a carp and decided not to write about it.   *Guindon cartoon caption*

362

All writing is garbage.

French playwright Antonin Artaud (1896–1948)

363

Novelists who go to psychiatrists are paying for what they should be paid for.   *Unknown*

364

Every author, however modest, keeps a most outrageous vanity chained like a madman in the padded cell of his breast.   *Logan Pearsall Smith (1865–1946)*

365

The trouble with our younger writers is that they are all in their sixties.   *W. Somerset Maugham (1874–1965)*

366

Authors are easy to get on with—if you like children.

Michael Joseph (1897–1958)

367

I write fiction because it's a way of making statements I can disown, and I write plays because dialogue is the most respectable way of contradicting myself.

Tom Stoppard

368

An essayist is a lucky person who has found a way to discourse without being interrupted.

Charles Poore

369
Writers aren't exactly people . . . they're a whole lot of people trying to be one person.

F. Scott Fitzgerald (1896–1940)

370
An author's first duty is to let down his country.

Brendan Behan (1923–1964)

371
Asking a working writer what he thinks about critics is like asking a lamp-post how it feels about dogs.

Christopher Hampton

372
I can't read ten pages of Steinbeck without throwing up.

James Gould Cozzens (1903–1978)

373
A poem is never finished, only abandoned.

Paul Valéry (1871–1945)

374
Immature poets imitate; mature poets steal.

T. S. Eliot (1888–1965)

375
Good swiping is an art in itself.

Jules Feiffer

376
Finishing a book is just like you took a child out in the back yard and shot it.

Truman Capote (1924–1984)

377
Dear Contributor: Thank you for not sending us anything lately. It suits our present needs.

Note from publisher received by Snoopy in comic strip "Peanuts" (Charles Schulz)

378
You call this a script? Give me a couple of 5,000-dollar-a-week writers and I'll write it myself.

Movie producer Joe Pasternak

379
I do most of my writing sitting down. That's where I shine.

Robert Benchley (1889–1945)

380
When in doubt, have two guys come through the door with guns.

Raymond Chandler (1888–1959)

381

Too many pieces of music finish too long after the end.

Igor Stravinsky (1882–1971)

382

My music is best understood by children and animals.

Igor Stravinsky (1882–1971)

383

You want something by Bach? Which one, Johann Sebastian or Jacques Offen?

Victor Borge

384

Even Bach comes down to the basic suck, blow, suck, suck, blow.   *Mouth organist Larry Adler*

385

Classical music is the kind we keep thinking will turn into a tune.   *Kin Hubbard (1868–1930)*

386

Opera in English is, in the main, just about as sensible as baseball in Italian.   *H. L. Mencken (1880–1956)*

387

I tried to resist his overtures, but he plied me with symphonies, quartettes, chamber music, and cantatas.

S. J. Perelman (1904–1979)

388
Anything that is too stupid to be spoken is sung.

Voltaire (1694–1778)

389
Massenet
Never wrote a Mass in A.
It'd have been just too bad
If he had.

Anthony Butts

390
No statue has ever been put up to a critic.

Jean Sibelius (1865–1957)

391
Music played at weddings always reminds me of the music
played for soldiers before they go into battle.

Heinrich Heine (1797–1856)

392
I don't know anything about music. In my line you don't have
to.   *Elvis Presley (1935–1977)*

393

Hell is full of musical amateurs.

George Bernard Shaw (1856–1950)

394

No sane man will dance. *Cicero (106–43 B.C.)*

395
Rock and roll is the hamburger that ate the world.
Peter York

396

Use an accordion, go to jail! That's the law!

Bumper sticker

397

You can make a killing as a playwright in America, but you can't make a living.

Sherwood Anderson (1876–1941)

398

All playwrights should be dead for three hundred years.

Joseph L. Mankiewicz

399

Actresses will happen in the best regulated families.

Oliver Herford (1863–1935)

400

My tears stuck in their little ducts, refusing to be jerked.

Peter Stack in a movie review

401

His performance is so wooden you want to spray him with Liquid Pledge.

John Stark in a movie review

402

Working in the theater has a lot in common with unemployment.

Arthur Gingold

403

Only in show business could a guy with a C-minus average be considered an intellectual.

Mort Sahl on himself

404

I don't want to see the uncut version of anything.

Jean Kerr

405

It's always easier to see a show you don't like the second time because you know it ends.

Walter Slezak (1902–1983)

406

Hell is a half-filled auditorium.

Robert Frost (1874–1963)

407

A critic is a man who knows the way but can't drive the car.

Kenneth Tynan (1927–1980)

408

Hollywood is a place where they place you under contract instead of under observation.

Walter Winchell (1897–1972)

409

The Hollywood tradition I like best is called "sucking up to the stars."

Johnny Carson

410

"Hello," he lied.

Don Carpenter quoting a Hollywood agent

411

An associate producer is the only guy in Hollywood who will associate with a producer.

Fred Allen (1894–1956)

412

The dead actor requested in his will that his body be cremated and ten percent of his ashes thrown in his agent's face.

Unknown

413

It was like passing the scene of a highway accident and being relieved to learn that nobody had been seriously injured.

Martin Cruz Smith on being asked how he liked the movie version of his novel Gorky Park

414

If you want to make it in show business, get the hell out of Oregon.

Advice from Sophie Tucker (1884–1966) to a young Johnnie Ray

415

Television has proved that people will look at anything rather than each other.

Ann Landers

416

Television is more interesting than people. If it were not, we would have people standing in the corners of our rooms.

Alan Corenk

417

Television is a medium because anything well done is rare.
Fred Allen (1894–1956)

418

Your picture tube is okay, but your cabinet has Dutch elm
disease.   *TV repairman in a Ziggy cartoon*

419

I'm So Miserable Without You
It's Almost Like Having You Here
Stephen Bishop song title

420

She Got the Gold Mine, I Got the Shaft
Jerry Reed song title

421

When My Love Comes Back from the Ladies' Room Will I Be
Too Old to Care?
Lewis Grizzard song title

422
I Don't Know Whether to Kill Myself or Go Bowling
Song title by Unknown

423
Why won't you lemme feelya, Cecilia?
I got two winnin' hands I wanna dealya.
Lyrics by Robert Byrne

424
They Tore Out My Heart and Stomped That Sucker Flat
Book title by Lewis Grizzard

425
[Americans] are a race of convicts and ought to be thankful
for anything we allow them short of hanging.
Samuel Johnson (1709–1784)

426
America is a large friendly dog in a small room. Every time
it wags its tail it knocks over a chair.
Arnold Toynbee (1889–1975)

427
The United States is like the guy at the party who gives
cocaine to everybody and still nobody likes him.
Jim Samuels

428

In America there are two classes of travel—first and with children.   *Robert Benchley (1889–1945)*

429

On Thanksgiving Day all over America, families sit down to dinner at the same moment—halftime.

Unknown

430

Animals have these advantages over man: they never hear the clock strike, they die without any idea of death, they have no theologians to instruct them, their last moments are not disturbed by unwelcome and unpleasant ceremonies, their funerals cost them nothing, and no one starts lawsuits over their wills.   *Voltaire (1694–1778)*

431

A boy can learn a lot from a dog: obedience, loyalty, and the importance of turning around three times before lying down.   *Robert Benchley (1889–1945)*

432

Man is the only animal that can remain on friendly terms with the victims he intends to eat until he eats them.
                              Samuel Butler (1835–1902)

433

Fox hunting is the unspeakable in pursuit of the inedible.
                              Oscar Wilde (1856–1900)

434

If you are a police dog, where's your badge?
*The question James Thurber (1894–1961) used to drive his
                              German shepherd crazy*

435

I loathe people who keep dogs. They are cowards who haven't got the guts to bite people themselves.
                              August Strindberg (1849–1912)

436

People on horses look better than they are, people in cars look worse.
Marya Mannes

437

We tolerate shapes in human beings that would horrify us if we saw them in a horse.
W. R. Inge (1860–1954)

438

You're a good example of why some animals eat their young.
Jim Samuels to a heckler

439

Cats are intended to teach us that not everything in nature has a function.
Garrison Keillor

440

Groundhog Day has been observed only once in Los Angeles because when the groundhog came out of its hole, it was killed by a mud slide.
Johnny Carson

441

Is that a beard, or are you eating a muskrat?

Dr. Gonzo

442

To err is human
To purr feline.

Robert Byrne

443

It isn't easy being green.

Kermit the Frog

444

Never go to a doctor whose office plants have died.

Erma Bombeck

445

Three out of four doctors recommend another doctor.

Graffito

446

I suppose one has a greater sense of intellectual degradation after an interview with a doctor than from any human experience. *Alice James (1848–1892)*

447

A young doctor means a new graveyard.

German proverb

448

I'm going to Boston to see my doctor. He's a very sick man.

Fred Allen (1894–1956)

449

People who take cold baths never have rheumatism, but they have cold baths.   *Unknown*

450

His ideas of first-aid stopped short of squirting soda water.
P. G. Wodehouse (1881–1975)

451

Before undergoing a surgical operation, arrange your temporal affairs. You may live.

Ambrose Bierce (1842–1914?)

452
Psychoanalysis is that mental illness for which it regards itself a therapy.   *Karl Kraus (1874–1936)*

453
Show me a sane man and I will cure him for you.
                                                  C. G. Jung (1875–1961)

454
Psychiatry is the care of the id by the odd.
                                                              Unknown

455
After twelve years of therapy my psychiatrist said something that brought tears to my eyes. He said, *"No hablo inglés."*
                                                           Ronnie Shakes

456
Doctors and lawyers must go to school for years and years, often with little sleep and with great sacrifice to their first wives.   *Roy G. Blount, Jr.*

457
I never did give anybody hell. I just told the truth and they thought it was hell.
                                                  Harry S Truman (1884–1972)

458

I can think of nothing more boring for the American people than to have to sit in their living rooms for a whole half hour looking at my face on their television screens.

Dwight David Eisenhower (1890–1969)

459

Do you realize the responsibility I carry? I'm the only person standing between Nixon and the White House.

John F. Kennedy (1917–1963), in 1960

460

I'm not sure I've even got the brains to be President.

Barry Goldwater in 1964

461

I would not like to be a political leader in Russia. They never know when they're being taped.

Richard Nixon

462

I love America. You always hurt the one you love.

David Frye impersonating Nixon

463

The thought of being President frightens me and I do not think I want the job.

Ronald Reagan in 1973

464

God! The country that produced George Washington has got this collection of crumb-bums!

Barbara Tuchman on the 1980 presidential candidates

465

Reagan won because he ran against Jimmy Carter. Had he run unopposed he would have lost.

Mort Sahl

466

Ronald Reagan is a triumph of the embalmer's art.

Gore Vidal

467

Ronald Reagan's platform seems to be: Hey, I'm a big good-looking guy and I need a lot of sleep.

Roy G. Blount, Jr.

468

Walter Mondale has all the charisma of a speed bump.

Will Durst

469

You've got to be careful quoting Ronald Reagan, because when you quote him accurately it's called mudslinging.

Walter Mondale

470

Women are being considered as candidates for Vice President of the United States because it is the worst job in America. It's amazing that men will take it. A job with real power is First Lady. I'd be willing to run for that. As far as the men who are running for President are concerned, they aren't even people I would date.

Nora Ephron

471

The man with the best job in the country is the Vice President. All he has to do is get up every morning and say, "How's the President?"

Will Rogers (1879–1935)

472

The vice-presidency ain't worth a pitcher of warm spit.

Vice President John Nance Garner (1868–1967)

473

If it were not for the government, we would have nothing to laugh at in France.

Sébastian Chamfort (1740–1794)

474

Every decent man is ashamed of the government he lives under.

H. L. Mencken (1880–1956)

475

It has been said that democracy is the worst form of government except all the others that have been tried.

Winston Churchill (1874–1965)

476

Democracy substitutes election by the incompetent many for appointment by the corrupt few.

George Bernard Shaw (1856–1950)

477

Get all the fools on your side and you can be elected to anything.

Frank Dane

478

If voting changed anything, they'd make it illegal.

Unknown

479

Vote early and vote often.

Al Capone (1899–1947)

480

Ninety percent of the politicians give the other ten percent a bad reputation.

Henry Kissinger

481

Politics is applesauce.

Will Rogers (1879–1935)

482

I might have gone to West Point, but I was too proud to speak to a congressman.

Will Rogers (1879–1935)

483

An ambassador is an honest man sent abroad to lie for his country.   *Sir Henry Wotton (1568–1639)*

484

A statesman is a politician who has been dead ten or fifteen years.   *Harry S Truman (1884–1972)*

485

Right in the middle of Prague, Wenceslaus Square, there's this guy throwing up. And this other guy comes along, takes a look at him, shakes his head, and says, "I know just what you mean."   *Milan Kundera*

486

When you go into court you are putting your fate into the hands of twelve people who weren't smart enough to get out of jury duty.   *Norm Crosby*

487

Getting kicked out of the American Bar Association is like getting kicked out of the Book-of-the-Month Club.

Melvin Belli on the occasion of
his getting kicked out of the American Bar Association

488

Laws are like sausages. It's better not to see them being made. *Otto von Bismarck (1815–1898)*

489

I always turn to the sports pages first, which record people's accomplishments. The front page has nothing but man's failures. *Chief Justice Earl Warren (1891–1974)*

490

I was not successful as a ballplayer, as it was a game of skill. *Casey Stengel (1891–1975)*

491

It matters not whether you win or lose; what matters is whether *I* win or lose.

Darin Weinberg

492

I'm glad we don't have to play in the shade. *Golfer Bobby Jones (1902–1971) on being told that it was 105 degrees in the shade*

493

Very few blacks will take up golf until the requirement for plaid pants is dropped.

Franklyn Ajaye

494

San Francisco has always been my favorite booing city. I don't mean the people boo louder or longer, but there is a very special intimacy. When they boo you, you know they mean *you*. Music, that's what it is to me. One time in Kezar Stadium they gave me a standing boo.

Pro football coach George Halas (1895–1983)

495

Most weightlifters are biceptual.

John Rostoni

496

I never met a man I didn't want to fight.

Pro football lineman Lyle Alzado

Part III

Miscellaneous

497

If politicians and scientists were lazier, how much happier
we should all be.

Evelyn Waugh (1903–1966)

498

If we see the light at the end of the tunnel
It's the light of an oncoming train.

Robert Lowell (1917–1977)

499

Ninety percent of everything is crap.

Theodore Sturgeon

500

You've always made the mistake of being yourself.

Eugène Ionesco

501

There is such a build-up of crud in my oven there is only
room to bake a single cupcake.

Phyllis Diller

502

Cleaning your house while your kids are still growing is like
shoveling the walk before it stops snowing.

Phyllis Diller

503

All phone calls are obscene.

Karen Elizabeth Gordon

504

There is no need to do any housework at all. After the first four years the dirt doesn't get any worse.

Quentin Crisp

505

Coincidences are spiritual puns.

G. K. Chesterton (1874–1936)

506

If I had to live my life again, I'd make the same mistakes, only sooner. *Tallulah Bankhead (1903–1968)*

507

Last night I dreamed I ate a ten-pound marshmallow, and when I woke up the pillow was gone.

Tommy Cooper

508

It's better to be wanted for murder than not to be wanted at all. *Marty Winch*

509

I have a hundred times wished that one could resign life as an officer resigns a commission.

Robert Burns (1759–1796)

510

The more he talked of his honor the faster we counted our spoons.   *Ralph Waldo Emerson (1803–1882)*

511

If you tell the truth you don't have to remember anything.
                    Mark Twain (1835–1910)

512

The truth is the safest lie.   *Anonymous*

513
No one can have a higher opinion of him than I have, and I think he's a dirty little beast.

W. S. Gilbert (1836–1911)

514
The future is much like the present, only longer.

Don Quisenberry

515
Advertising is the rattling of a stick inside a swill bucket.

George Orwell (1903–1950)

516
Winter is nature's way of saying, "Up yours."

Robert Byrne

517
I like winter because I can stay indoors without feeling guilty.

Teressa Skelton

518
Weather forecast for tonight: dark.

George Carlin

519
If I were two-faced, would I be wearing this one?

Abraham Lincoln (1809–1865)

520

A person can take only so much comforting.

Calvin Trillin

521

I have a rock garden. Last week three of them died.

Richard Diran

522

Nice guys finish last, but we get to sleep in.

Evan Davis

523

Illegal aliens have always been a problem in the United States. Ask any Indian.

Robert Orben

524

Few things are harder to put up with than a good example.

Mark Twain (1835–1910)

525

I just got wonderful news from my real estate agent in Florida. They found land on my property.

Milton Berle

526

Immigration is the sincerest form of flattery.

Jack Paar

527

The art of living is more like wrestling than dancing.

Marcus Aurelius (121–180)

528

We must believe in luck. For how else can we explain the success of those we don't like?

Jean Cocteau (1889–1963)

529

Hell is other people.

Jean Paul Sartre (1905–1980)

530

Some people are always late, like the late King George V.

Spike Milligan

531

It is easier to get forgiveness than permission.

Stewart's Law of Retroaction in
Murphy's Law, Book Two

532

The popularity of a bad man is as treacherous as he is
himself. *Pliny the Younger (c. 62–c. 113)*

533

The hatred of relatives is the most violent.

Tacitus (c.55–c. 117)

534

Every man sees in his relatives a series of grotesque carica-
tures of himself. *H. L. Mencken (1880–1956)*

535

The first Rotarian was the first man to call John the Baptist
"Jack." *H. L. Mencken (1880–1956)*

536

Even if you're on the right track, you'll get run over if you just sit there.   *Will Rogers (1879–1935)*

537

H. L. Mencken suffers from the hallucination that he is H. L. Mencken. There is no cure for a disease of that magnitude.
          Maxwell Bodenhein (1893–1954)

538

I prefer rogues to imbeciles because they sometimes take a rest.   *Alexandre Dumas the Younger (1824–1895)*

539
A wedding cake left out in the rain.
*Stephen Spender commenting on
the face of W. H. Auden (1907–1973)*

540
Is this the party to whom I am speaking?
Lily Tomlin as Ernestine the operator

541
Let others praise ancient times; I am glad I was born in these.
Ovid (43 B.C.–A.D. *18)*

542
Happiness is good health and a bad memory.
Ingrid Bergman (1917–1982)

543
Never keep up with the Joneses. Drag them down to your
level.
Quentin Crisp

544
People who think they know everything are very irritating to
those of us who do.
Unknown

545

I want a house that has got over all its troubles; I don't want to spend the rest of my life bringing up a young and inexperienced house.

Jerome K. Jerome (1859–1927)

546

There is something about a closet that makes a skeleton restless. *Unknown*

547

By dint of railing at idiots you run the risk of becoming idiotic yourself.

Gustave Flaubert (1821–1880)

548

There is no gravity. The earth sucks.

Graffito

549

When the going gets tough, the smart get lost.

Robert Byrne

550

Miss Erickson looked more peculiar than ever this morning. Is her spiritualism getting worse?

Noel Coward (1889–1973)

551

I shot an arrow into the air, and it stuck.

Graffito in Los Angeles

552

There's so much pollution in the air now that if it weren't for our lungs there'd be no place to put it all.

Robert Orben

553

I don't know how old I am because the goat ate the Bible that had my birth certificate in it. The goat lived to be twenty-seven.
Satchel Paige (1906?-1982)

554

Nothing ever goes away.
Barry Commoner

555

There's nothing wrong with you that reincarnation won't cure.
Jack E. Leonard (1911-1973)
to Ed Sullivan (1902-1974)

556

A lie is an abomination unto the Lord and a very present help in time of trouble.
Adlai Stevenson (1900-1965)

557

During a carnival men put masks over their masks.
Xavier Forneret, 1838

558

One hundred thousand lemmings can't be wrong.
Graffito

559
He was the world's only armless sculptor. He put the chisel in his mouth and his wife hit him on the back of the head with a mallet. *Fred Allen (1894–1956)*

560
Modern art is what happens when painters stop looking at girls and persuade themselves that they have a better idea.
John Ciardi

561
Either this wallpaper goes or I do.
Almost certainly not the last words of Oscar Wilde (1856–1900)

562
A life spent making mistakes is not only more honorable but more useful than a life spent doing nothing.
George Bernard Shaw (1856–1950)

563
Friends may come and go, but enemies accumulate.
Thomas Jones

564
When down in the mouth, remember Jonah. He came out all right. *Thomas Edison (1847–1931)*

565

Retirement at sixty-five is ridiculous. When I was sixty-five I still had pimples. *George Burns*

566

Old age is the only disease you don't look forward to being cured of. *From the movie* Citizen Kane, *1941*

567

Start every day off with a smile and get it over with. *W. C. Fields (1880–1946)*

568

I took a course in speed reading and was able to read *War and Peace* in twenty minutes. It's about Russia. *Woody Allen*

569

When your IQ rises to 28, sell. *Professor Irwin Corey to a heckler*

570

Some people are like popular songs that you only sing for a short time. *La Rochefoucauld (1613–1680)*

571

George the Third
Ought never to have occurred.
One can only wonder
At so grotesque a blunder.

Edmund Clerihew (1875–1956)

572

There are two kinds of pedestrians . . . the quick and the
dead. *Lord Thomas Robert Dewar (1864–1930)*

573

I used to work in a fire hydrant factory. You couldn't park
anywhere near the place.

Steven Wright

574

I don't have any trouble parking. I drive a forklift.

Jim Samuels

575

God help those who do not help themselves.

Wilson Mizner (1876–1933)

576

There is only one good substitute for the endearments of a
sister, and that is the endearments of some other fellow's
sister. *Josh Billings (1818–1885)*

577

When smashing monuments, save the pedestals—they always come in handy.

Stanislaw Lem

578

Great men are not always idiots.

Karen Elizabeth Gordon

579
Few great men could pass Personnel.

Paul Goodman (1911–1972)

580
Fanaticism consists of redoubling your effort when you have forgotten your aim.

George Santayana (1863–1952)

581
Mountains appear more lofty the nearer they are approached, but great men resemble them not in this particular.

Lady Marguerite Blessington (1789–1849)

582
There's a great woman behind every idiot.

John Lennon (1941–1980) on Yoko Ono

583
Nothing is more conducive to peace of mind than not having any opinions at all.

Georg Christoph Lichtenberg (1742–1799)

584
The mome rath isn't born that could outgrabe me.

Nicol Williamson

585
If you live to the age of a hundred you have it made because very few people die past the age of a hundred.

George Burns

586
Never accept an invitation from a stranger unless he gives you candy.

Linda Festa

587
You can choose your friends, but you only have one mother.

Max Shulman

588
One is not superior merely because one sees the world as odious.

Chateaubriand (1768–1848)

589
If it weren't for the last minute, nothing would get done.

Unknown

590
If I were a grave-digger or even a hangman, there are some people I could work for with a great deal of enjoyment.

Douglas Jerrold (1803–1857)

591
It is easier to forgive an enemy than to forgive a friend.

William Blake (1757–1827)

592

You are no bigger than the things that annoy you.

Jerry Bundsen

593

It is unpleasant to go alone, even to be drowned.

Russian proverb

594

Stay with me; I want to be alone.

Joey Adams

595

They made love only during total eclipses of the sun because they wouldn't take off their clothes unless it was dark in the entire world.   *Unknown*

596

We are what we pretend to be.

Kurt Vonnegut, Jr.

597

Thank you, but I have other plans.
Response to "Have a nice day" suggested by Paul Fussell

598

WARNING TO ALL PERSONNEL
Firings will continue until moral improves.

Unknown

599

Do we really deserve top billing?
*Fred Allen (1894–1956) to Henry Morgan
at a meeting of the National Conference
of Christians and Jews*

600

Psychics will lead dogs to your body.
Alleged fortune cookie message

601

I don't worry about crime in the streets; it's the sidewalks I stay off of.   *Johnson Letellier*

602

Carney's Law: There's at least a 50-50 chance that someone will print the name Craney incorrectly.

Jim Canrey

603

Bad spellers of the world, untie!

Graffito

604

Complete this sentence:
   I never met a man I didn't like
     a. to cheat.
     b. at first.
     c. to avoid.
     d. better than you.

Robert Byrne

605

Fix this sentence:
   He put the horse before the cart.

Stephen Price

606

I am firm. You are obstinate. He is a pig-headed fool.

Katharine Whitehorn

607

Dr. Livingstone I Presume
        Full name of Dr. Presume

Unknown

608

A language is a dialect with an army and navy.

Max Weinreich (1894–1969)

609

I can't seem to bring myself to say, "Well, I guess I'll be toddling along." It isn't that I can't toddle. It's that I can't guess I'll toddle.

Robert Benchley (1889–1945)

610

Hamlet as performed at the Brooklyn Shakespeare Festival:
        "To be, or what?"

Steven Pearl

611

Smoking is, as far as I'm concerned, the entire point of being an adult.
Fran Lebowitz

612

A steam engine has always got character. It's the most human of all man-made machines.

Reverend William Vere Awdrey

613

There is only one word for aid that is genuinely without strings, and that word is blackmail.

Colm Brogan

614

Al didn't smile for forty years. You've got to admire a man like that.

From the television series
"Mary Hartman, Mary Hartman"

615

All professions are conspiracies against the laity.

George Bernard Shaw (1856–1950)

616

Very few people do anything creative after the age of thirty-five. The reason is that very few people do anything creative before the age of thirty-five.

Joel Hildebrand (1881–1983)

617

There is no they, only us.

Bumper sticker

618

I was in a beauty contest once. I not only came in last, I was hit in the mouth by Miss Congeniality.

Phyllis Diller

619

You can get more with a kind word and a gun than you can with a kind word alone.

Johnny Carson

620

I think it would be a good idea.

Mahatma Gandhi (1869–1948) when asked what he thought of Western civilization

621

Remember that a kick in the ass is a step forward.

Unknown

622

What is algebra, exactly? Is it those three-cornered things?

J. M. Barrie (1860-1937)

623

Computers are useless. They can only give you answers.

Pablo Picasso (1881-1973)

624

Peace, n. In international affairs, a period of cheating between two periods of fighting.

Ambrose Bierce (1842-1914?)

625

Let thy maid servant be faithful, strong, and homely.

Benjamin Franklin (1706-1790)

626

At twenty-six, Kate, though not promiscuous, had slept with most of the decent men in public life.

Renata Adler

627

The egg cream is psychologically the opposite of circumcision—it *pleasurably* reaffirms your Jewishness.

Mel Brooks

628

His absence is good company.

Scottish saying

629

The happiest liaisons are based on mutual misunderstanding.
La Rochefoucauld (1613–1680)

630

So many beautiful women and so little time.
John Barrymore (1882–1942)

631

The art of *not* reading is extremely important. It consists in our not taking up whatever happens to occupy the larger public.   *Arthur Schopenhauer (1788–1860)*

632

Nowadays the illiterates can read and write.
Alberto Moravia

633

A good man is always a beginner.
Martial (c. 40–c. 104)

634

I knew a very interesting Italian woman last winter, but now she's married.
Percy Bysshe Shelley (1792–1822)

635

How much money did you make last year? Mail it in.
Simplified tax form suggested by Stanton Delaplane

636

Gray hair is God's graffiti.

Bill Cosby

637

The gods too are fond of a joke.

Aristotle (384–322 B.C.)

The Third
and Possibly
the Best
637 Best Things
Anybody Ever Said

For
Susan Richman
The best in the business

Part I

Religion, Life Itself, Men and Women, Cats, Clothes, Love, Sex, Marriage, Self-Abuse, Parents, Kids, Work, Money, Crime, Old Age, Death and one thing and another

1

The only thing that stops God from sending another flood is that the first one was useless.

Nicholas Chamfort (1741–1794)

2

The world is proof that God is a committee.

Bob Stokes

3

God is dead, but fifty thousand social workers have risen to take his place.

J.D. McCoughey

4

Which is it, is man one of God's blunders or is God one of man's?

Friedrich Nietzsche (1844–1900)

5

Nietzsche was stupid and abnormal.

Leo Tolstoy (1818–1910)

6

Millions long for immortality who don't know what to do on a rainy Sunday afternoon.

Susan Ertz

7

A pious man is one who would be an athiest if the king were.

Jean de La Bruyère (1645–1696)

8

I detest converts almost as much as I do missionaries.
H.L. Mencken (1880–1956)

9

Most of my friends are not Christians, but I have some who are Anglicans or Roman Catholics.
Dame Rose Macaulay (1881–1958)

10

Promise me that if you become a Christian you'll become a Presbyterian.
Lord Beaverbrook (1879–1964) to Josef Stalin in 1941

11

The history of saints is mainly the history of insane people.
Benito Mussolini (1883–1945)

12

In Burbank there's a drive-in church called Jack-in-the-Pew. You shout your sins into the face of a plastic priest.
Johnny Carson

13

When I was a kid in the ghetto, a gang started going around harassing people, so some of the toughest kids formed a gang called The Sharks to stop them. The other gang was called The Jehovah's Witnesses.
Charles Kosar

14

Jesus was a Jew, yes, but only on his mother's side.

Stanley Ralph Ross

15

Unless you hate your father and mother and wife and brothers and sisters and, yes, even your own life, you can't be my disciple.

Jesus Christ (0?–32?), if St. Luke is to be believed.
See Luke 14:26.

16

Jesus was a crackpot.

Bhagwan Shree Rajneesh

17

Let Bhagwans be Bhagwans.

Headline considered by the Washington Post

18

Jesus died too soon. If he had lived to my age he would have repudiated his doctrine.

Friedrich Nietzsche (1844–1900)

Nietzsche was stupid and abnormal.

Leo Tolstoy (1828–1910)

19

I'm not going to climb into the ring with Tolstoy.

Ernest Hemingway (1898–1961)

20

Hemingway was a jerk.

Harold Robbins

21

The purpose of life is a life of purpose.

Robert Byrne

22

I like life. It's something to do.

Ronnie Shakes

23

Life is divided into the horrible and the miserable.

Woody Allen

24

Life is just a bowl of pits.

Rodney Dangerfield

25

Life being what it is, one dreams of revenge.

Paul Gauguin (1848–1903)

26

If I had my life to live over, I'd live over a delicatessen.

Unknown

27

Man is more an ape than many of the apes.

Friedrich Nietzsche (1844–1900)

Neitzsche was stupid and abnormal.

Leo Tolstoy (1828–1910)

28

He who looketh upon a woman loseth a fender.

Sign in auto repair shop

29

Mahatma Gandhi was what wives wish their husbands were: thin, tan, and moral.

Unknown

30

The only time a woman really succeeds in changing a man is when he's a baby.

Natalie Wood (1938–1981)

31

I'm a disgrace to my sex. I should work in an Arabian palace as a eunuch.

Woody Allen

32

Girls are always running through my mind. They don't dare walk.

Andy Gibb

33

One good thing about being a man is that men don't have to talk to each other. *Peter Cocotas*

34

Of all the wild beasts of land or sea, the wildest is woman. *Menander (342?–291? B.C.)*

35

A woman is always buying something. *Ovid (43 B.C.–A.D. 18)*

36

Nothing is more intolerable than a wealthy woman. *Juvenal (60?–140?)*

37

A woman talks to one man, looks at a second, and thinks of a third. *Bhartrihari, ca. 625*

38

Woman was God's second mistake. *Friedrich Nietzsche (1844–1900)*

Nietzsche was stupid and abnormal. *Leo Tolstoy (1828–1910)*

39

Women speak two languages, one of which is verbal. *Steve Rubenstein*

40

Women who seek to be equal with men lack ambition. *Timothy Leary*

41

Women are like elephants to me. I like to look at them but
I wouldn't want to own one.

W.C. Fields (1880–1946)

42

Phyllis Schlafly speaks for all American women who oppose equal rights for themselves.

Andy Rooney

43

Housework can kill you if done right.

Erma Bombeck

44

What do women want? Shoes.

Mimi Pond

45

Shopping tip: You can get shoes for 85 cents at bowling alleys.   *Al Clethen*

46

Can you imagine a world without men? No crime and lots of happy fat women.

Sylvia (Nicole Hollander)

47

Veni, vidi, Visa. *(We came, we saw, we went shopping.)*

Jan Barrett

48

Any girl can be glamorous; all you have to do is stand still and look stupid.   *Hedy Lamarr*

49

If they could put one man on the moon, why can't they put them all?   *Unknown*

50

Good breeding consists of concealing how much we think of ourselves and how little we think of the other person.

Mark Twain (1835–1910)

51

Charm is a way of getting the answer yes without asking a clear question.   *Albert Camus (1913–1960)*

52

Good taste is the worst vice ever invented.

Dame Edith Sitwell (1887–1964)

53

We are all born charming, fresh, and spontaneous and must be civilized before we are fit to participate in society.

Miss Manners (Judith Martin)

54

Cats are smarter than dogs. You can't get eight cats to pull a sled through snow. *Jeff Valdez*

55

Dogs come when they're called; cats take a message and get back to you. *Mary Bly*

56

If a cat spoke, it would say things like "Hey, I don't see the *problem* here." *Roy Blount, Jr.*

57

A man who was loved by 300 women singled me out to live with him. Why? I was the only one without a cat.

Elayne Boosler

58

I take my pet lion to church every Sunday. He has to eat.

Marty Pollio

59

Cute rots the intellect.

Garfield (Jim Davis)

60

Distrust any enterprise that requires new clothes.

Henry David Thoreau (1817–1862)

61

Fashions are induced epidemics.

George Bernard Shaw (1856–1950)

62

You'd be surprised how much it costs to look this cheap.

Dolly Parton

63

There is a new awareness of style in the Soviet Union. The premier's wife recently appeared on the cover of *House and Tractor.*

Johnny Carson

64

I should warn you that underneath these clothes I'm wearing boxer shorts and I know how to use them.

Robert Orben

65

What you have when everyone wears the same playclothes for all occasions, is addressed by nickname, expected to participate in Show and Tell, and bullied out of any desire for privacy, is not democracy; it is kindergarten.

Miss Manners (Judith Martin)

66

Being named as one of the world's best-dressed men doesn't necessarily mean that I am a bad person.

Anthony R. Cucci, Mayor of Jersey City

67

In love there are two evils: war and peace.

Horace (65–8 B.C.)

68

Love is the crocodile on the river of desire.

Bhartrihari (ca. 625)

69

Love is what happens to men and women who don't know each other.

W. Somerset Maugham (1874–1965)

70

Love is blond.

Herbert Gold's mother

71

The trouble with loving is that pets don't last long enough and people last too long.

Unknown

72

A man always remembers his first love with special tenderness, but after that he begins to bunch them.

H.L. Mencken (1880–1956)

73

When you are in love with someone you want to be near him all the time, except when you are out buying things and charging them to him.

Miss Piggy, according to Henry Beard,
Miss Piggy's Guide to Life, *1981*

74

Better to have loved and lost a short person than never to have loved a tall. *David Chambless*

75

One of the advantages of living alone is that you don't have to wake up in the arms of a loved one.

Marion Smith

76

Dear Sweetheart:
Last night I thought of you.
At least I think it was you.

Love letter by Snoopy (Charles Schulz)

77

In the race for love, I was scratched.

Joan Davis (1912–1961)

78

Outside every thin woman is a fat man trying to get in.

Katherine Whitehorn

79

Sex is natural, but not if it's done right.

Unknown

80

Sex is good, but not as good as fresh sweet corn.

Garrison Keillor

81

There is hardly anyone whose sexual life, if it were broadcast, would not fill the world at large with surprise and horror. *W. Somerset Maugham (1874–1965)*

82

There is nothing a young man can get by wenching but duels, the clap, and bastards.

Kathleen Winsor

83

It is more fun contemplating somebody else's navel than your own.   *Arthur Hoppe*

84

Of all the sexual aberrations, perhaps the most peculiar is chastity.   *Remy de Gourmont (1858–1915)*

85

We may eventually come to realize that chastity is no more a virtue than malnutrition.

Alex Comfort

86

I used to be a virgin, but I gave it up because there was no money in it.   *Marsha Warfield*

87

A terrible thing happened again last night—nothing.

Phyllis Diller

88

Celibacy is not hereditary.

Guy Goden

89

Kissing is a means of getting two people so close together that they can't see anything wrong with each other.

René Yasenek

90

Oh, what lies there are in kisses!

Heinrich Heine (1797–1856)

91

Whenever I'm caught between two evils, I take the one I've never tried.

Mae West (1892–1980)

92

It is better to copulate than never.

Robert Heinlein

93

Vasectomy means never having to say you're sorry.

Unknown

94

Last night I discovered a new form of oral contraceptive. I asked a girl to go to bed with me and she said no.

Woody Allen

95

I told my girl friend that unless she expressed her feelings and told me what she liked I wouldn't be able to please her, so she said, "Get off me."

Garry Shandling

96

She was so wild that when she made French toast she got her tongue caught in the toaster.

Rodney Dangerfield

97

I'm too shy to express my sexual needs except over the phone to people I don't know.

Garry Shandling

98

Sex Appeal—Give Generously

Bumper sticker

99

How did sex come to be thought of as dirty in the first place? God must have been a Republican.

Will Durst

100

Before we make love, my husband takes a pain killer.

Joan Rivers

101

My wife was in labor with our first child for thirty-two hours and I was faithful to her the whole time.

Jonathan Katz

102

My wife has cut our lovemaking down to once a month, but I know two guys she's cut out entirely.

Rodney Dangerfield

103

Chains required, whips optional.

California highway sign

104

The fantasy of every Australian man is to have two women —one cleaning and the other dusting.

Maureen Murphy

105

Ouch! You're on My Hair!

Sex manual title suggested by Richard Lewis

106

The difference between pornography and erotica is lighting.

Gloria Leonard

107

If homosexuality were normal, God would have created Adam and Bruce. *Anita Bryant*

108

Rub-a-dub-dub
Three men in a tub
And that's on a slow night.

Sign in a San Francisco bath house

109

Never play leapfrog with a unicorn.

Unknown

110

Get in good physical condition before submitting to bondage. You should be fit to be tied.

Robert Byrne

111

I caused my husband's heart attack. In the middle of love-making I took the paper bag off my head. He dropped the Polaroid and keeled over and so did the hooker. It would have taken me half an hour to untie myself and call the paramedics, but fortunately the Great Dane could dial.

Joan Rivers

112

A British mother's advice to her daughter on how to survive the wedding night: "Close your eyes and think of England."

Pierre Daninos

113

I have so little sex appeal that my gynecologist calls me "sir."

Joan Rivers

114

What men call gallantry and gods adultery
Is much more common where the climate's sultry.

Lord Byron (1788–1824)

115

Of all the tame beasts, I hate sluts.

John Ray (1627?–1705)

116

I'd like to have a girl, and I'm saving my money so I can get a good one.

Bob Nickman

117

A relationship is what happens between two people who are waiting for something better to come along.

Unknown

118

I have such poor vision I can date anybody.

Garry Shandling

119

It's relaxing to go out with my ex-wife because she already knows I'm an idiot.

Warren Thomas

120

I used to go out exclusively with actresses and other female impersonators.

Mort Sahl

121

The trouble with living in sin is the shortage of closet space.
Missy Dizick

122

The fickleness of the women I love is only equalled by the infernal constancy of the woman who love me.
George Bernard Shaw (1856–1950)

123

Burt Reynolds once asked me out. I was in his room.
Phyllis Diller

124

He's the kind of man a woman would have to marry to get rid of.
Mae West (1892–1980)

125

Brains are an asset, if you hide them.

Mae West (1892–1980)

126

He promised me earrings, but he only pierced my ears.

Arabian saying

127

Marriage is a necessary evil.

Menander (342?–291? B.C.)

128

Marriage is the only war in which you sleep with the enemy.

Unknown

129

Nothing anybody tells you about marriage helps.

Max Siegel

130

There is so little difference between husbands you might as well keep the first.

Adela Rogers St. Johns

131

Marriage is really tough because you have to deal with feelings and lawyers.   *Richard Pryor*

132

Marriage could catch on again because living together is not quite living and not quite together. Premarital sex slowly evolves into premarital sox.

Gerald Nachman

133

Marriage is part of a sort of 50's revival package that's back in vogue along with neckties and naked ambition.

Calvin Trillin

134

I'll have to marry a virgin. I can't stand criticism.

From the movie Out of Africa, *1985*

135

If you are living with a man, you don't have to worry about whether you should sleep with him after dinner.

Stephanie Brush

136

I'd like to get married because I like the idea of a man being required by law to sleep with me every night.

Carrie Snow

137

Alimony is like buying oats for a dead horse.

Arthur Baer (1896–1975)

138

I hated my marriage, but I always had a great place to park.

Gerald Nachman

139

Where I come from, when a Catholic marries a Lutheran it is considered the first step on the road to Minneapolis.

Garrison Keillor

140

I was married by a judge. I should have asked for a jury.

George Burns

141

I wouldn't trust my husband with a young woman for five minutes, and he's been dead for 25 years.

Brendan Behan's mother

142

I want a girl just like the girl that married dear old Dad.

Lyrics by Oedipus Rex

143

Adultery is a meanness and a stealing, a taking away from someone what should be theirs, a great selfishness, and surrounded and guarded by lies lest it should be found out. And out of the meanness and selfishness and lying flow love and joy and peace beyond anything that can be imagined.

Dame Rose Macaulay (1881–1958)

144

I am a marvelous housekeeper. Every time I leave a man I keep his house.

Zsa Zsa Gabor

145

The happiest time in any man's life is just after the first divorce.

John Kenneth Galbraith

146

One reason people get divorced is that they run out of gift ideas.

Robert Byrne

147

I've married a few people I shouldn't have, but haven't we all?

Mamie Van Doren

148

What I like about masturbation is that you don't have to talk afterwards. *Milos Forman*

149

If sex is so personal, why do we have to share it with someone? *Unknown*

150

Enjoy yourself. If you can't enjoy yourself, enjoy somebody else. *Jack Schaefer*

151

The only reason I feel guilty about masturbation is that I do it so badly. *David Steinberg*

152

Philip Roth is a good writer, but I wouldn't want to shake hands with him.

Jacqueline Susann (1921–1974)
after reading Portnoy's Complaint

153

I can't believe I forgot to have children.

Unknown

154

If God wanted sex to be fun, He wouldn't have included children as punishment.

Ed Bluestone

155

I am determined my children shall be brought up in their father's religion, if they can find out what it is.

Charles Lamb (1775–1834)

156

I could now afford all the things I never had as a kid, if I didn't have kids.   *Robert Orben*

157

My mother had a great deal of trouble with me, but I think she enjoyed it.   *Mark Twain (1835–1910)*

158

I'll probably never have children because I don't believe in touching people for any reason.

Paula Poundstone

159

I take my children everywhere, but they always find their way back home.   *Robert Orben*

160

My parents put a live teddy bear in my crib.

Woody Allen

161

I phoned my dad to tell him I had stopped smoking. He called me a quitter.

Steven Pearl

162

Never lend your car to anyone to whom you have given birth.

Erma Bombeck

163

The best revenge is to live long enough to be a problem to your children.

Unknown

164

Children today are tyrants. They contradict their parents, gobble their food, and tyrannize their teachers.

Socrates (470–399 B.C.)

165

An ugly baby is a very nasty object, and the prettiest is frightful when undressed.

Queen Victoria (1819–1901)

166

What is more enchanting than the voices of young people when you can't hear what they say?

Logan Pearsall Smith (1865–1946)

167

At my lemonade stand I used to give the first glass away free and charge five dollars for the second glass. The refill contained the antidote.

Emo Philips

168

When you are eight years old, nothing is any of your business.

Lenny Bruce (1926–1966)

169

What is youth except a man or woman before it is fit to be seen?

Evelyn Waugh (1903–1966)

170

My eleven-year-old daughter mopes around the house all day waiting for her breasts to grow.

Bill Cosby

171

If you're not beguiling by age twelve, forget it.

Lucy (Charles Schulz)

172

I was so naive as a kid I used to sneak behind the barn and do nothing.

Johnny Carson

173

My schoolmates would make love to anything that moved, but I never saw any reason to limit myself.

Emo Philips

174

I almost got a girl pregnant in high school. It's costing me a fortune to keep the rabbit on a life-support system.

Will Shriner

175

The trouble with the 1980's as compared with the 1970's is that teenagers no longer rebel and leave home.

Marion Smith

176

Learning to dislike children at an early age saves a lot of expense and aggravation later in life.

Robert Byrne

177

Adolescence is the stage between infancy and adultery.

Unknown

178

I like work; it fascinates me. I can sit and look at it for hours.

Jerome K. Jerome (1859–1927)

179

Work is for cowards.

Pool hustler U.J. Puckett in 1984 at age seventy-six

180
Always be smarter than the people who hire you.

Lena Horne

181
The trouble with unemployment is that the minute you wake up in the morning you're on the job.

Slappy White

182
The volume of paper expands to fill the available briefcases.

Jerry Brown

183
Any new venture goes through the following stages: enthusiasm, complication, disillusionment, search for the guilty, punishment of the innocent, and decoration of those who did nothing.

Unknown

184
When I realized that what I had turned out to be was a lousy, two-bit pool hustler and drunk, I wasn't depressed at all. I was glad to have a profession.

Danny McGoorty (1901–1970)

185

The reason American cities are prosperous is that there is no place to sit down. *Alfred J. Talley*

186

Gardner's Law: Eighty-seven percent of all people in all professions are incompetent.

John Gardner

187

It is time I stepped aside for a less experienced and less able man.

Professor Scott Elledge on his retirement from Cornell

188

The only way to succeed is to make people hate you.

Josef von Sternberg (1894–1969)

189

A man can't get rich if he takes proper care of his family.

Navajo saying

190

I believe that the power to make money is a gift from God.

John D. Rockefeller (1839–1937)

191

It is the wretchedness of being rich that you have to live with rich people.

Logan Pearsall Smith (1865–1946)

192

Never invest in anything that eats or needs repairing.

Billy Rose (1899–1966)

193

Every morning I get up and look through the Forbes list of the richest people in America. If I'm not there, I go to work.

Robert Orben

194

I enjoy being a highly overpaid actor.

Roger Moore

195

Buy old masters. They bring better prices than young mistresses. *Lord Beaverbrook (1879–1964)*

196

The income tax has made liars out of more Americans than golf. *Will Rogers (1879–1935)*

197

Why is there so much month left at the end of the money?

Unknown

198

Today you can go to a gas station and find the cash register open and the toilets locked. They must think toilet paper is worth more than money.

Joey Bishop

199

Enjoy money while you have it. Shrouds don't have pockets.

Virginia Esberg's grandmother

200

It is no disgrace to be poor, but it might as well be.

Jim Grue

201

So he's short . . . he can stand on his wallet.

Jewish mother

202

Business is a good game—lots of competition and a minimum of rules. You keep score with money.

Atari founder Nolan Bushnell

203

Economists are people who work with numbers but who don't have the personality to be accountants.

Unknown

204

An economist's guess is liable to be as good as anybody else's.

Will Rogers (1879–1935)

205

Mathematics has given economics rigor, but alas, also mortis.

Robert Heilbroner

206

Organized crime in America takes in over forty billion dollars a year and spends very little on office supplies.

Woody Allen

207

Getting caught is the mother of invention.

Robert Byrne

208

Capital punishment is either an affront to humanity or a potential parking place.

Larry Brown

209
I believe that people would be alive today if there were a death penalty.   *Nancy Reagan*

210
There is never enough time, unless you're serving it.
Malcolm Forbes

211
At age fifty, every man has the face he deserves.
George Orwell (1903–1950)

212
The secret of staying young is to live honestly, eat slowly, and lie about your age.   *Lucille Ball*

213
I am in the prime of senility.
Joel Chandler Harris (1848–1908) at age fifty-eight

214
I am not young enough to know everything.
Oscar Wilde (1854–1900)

215
The closing years of life are like the end of a masquerade party, when the masks are dropped.
Arthur Schopenhauer (1788–1860)

216

Old age is not for sissies.

Variously ascribed

217

Old age is when the liver spots show through your gloves.

Phyllis Diller

218

Old age is like a plane flying through a storm. Once you are aboard there is nothing you can do.

Golda Meir (1898–1978)

219

When I was young there was no respect for the young, and now that I am old there is no respect for the old. I missed out coming and going.

J.B. Priestley (1894–1984)

220

Middle age begins with the first mortgage and ends when you drop dead.

Herb Caen

221

You know you're old when you notice how young the derelicts are getting.

Jeanne Phillips

222

My grandfather used to make home movies and edit out the
joy.   *Richard Lewis*

223

I smoke cigars because at my age if I don't have something
to hang onto I might fall down.

George Burns

224

The hardest years in life are those between ten and seventy.

Helen Hayes at age eighty-three

225

After age seventy it's patch, patch, patch.

Jimmy Stewart

226

You have to be an antique to appreciate them.

Fay Madigan Lange

227

Death is just a distant rumor to the young.

Andy Rooney

228

They say such nice things about people at their funerals that it makes me sad to realize that I'm going to miss mine by just a few days.
Garrison Keillor

229

Big deal! I'm used to dust.
Gravestone epitaph requested by Erma Bombeck

230

There is no reason for me to die. I already died in Altoona.
George Burns

231
I know a man who gave up smoking, drinking, sex, and rich food. He was healthy right up to the time he killed himself.
Johnny Carson

232
The only thing wrong with immortality is that it tends to go on forever.
Herb Caen

233
There will be sex after death; we just won't be able to feel it.
Lily Tomlin

234
Dying ought to be done in black and white. It is simply not a colorful activity.
Russell Baker

235
What Einstein was to physics, what Babe Ruth was to home runs, what Emily Post was to table manners . . . that's what Edward G. Robinson was to dying like a dirty rat.
Russell Baker

Part II

Cynicism, Happiness, Morality, Bores, Food,
Doctors, Parties, Alcohol, Music, Sports, Art,
Law, Travel, Airplanes, Science, War, Movies,
Politics, Presidents, Writers and various odds
and ends

236

Idealism is what precedes experience; cynicism is what follows.   *David T. Wolf*

237

The cynics are right nine times out of ten.
                                        H. L. Mencken (1880–1956)

238

No matter how cynical you get, it is impossible to keep up.
                                                        Lily Tomlin

239

When there are two conflicting versions of a story, the wise course is to believe the one in which people appear at their worst.   *H. Allen Smith (1906–1976)*

240

Half the people in America are faking it.

                                                Robert Mitchum

241

Ignorance is the mother of admiration.
                                George Chapman (1599?–1634)

242

I was going to buy a copy of *The Power of Positive Thinking,*
and then I thought: What the hell good would that do?
                                                Ronnie Shakes

243

Nothing matters very much, and few things matter all.

Arthur Balfour (1848–1930)

244

Doing a thing well is often a waste of time.

Robert Byrne

245

Happiness is a Chinese meal; sorrow is a nourishment forever. *Carolyn Kizer*

246

There is no happiness; there are only moments of happiness.

Spanish proverb

247

I am a kind of paranoiac in reverse. I suspect people of plotting to make me happy.

J.D. Salinger

248

Happiness is having a large, loving, caring, close-knit family in another city. *George Burns*

249

O Lord, help me to be pure, but not yet.

St. Augustine (354–430)

250

An evil mind is a constant solace.

Unknown

251

A thing worth having is a thing worth cheating for.

W.C. Fields (1880–1946)

252

He without benefit of scruples
His fun and money soon quadruples.

Ogden Nash (1902–1971)

253

Living with a conscience is like driving a car with the brakes
on.   *Budd Schulberg*

254

In order to preserve your self-respect, it is sometimes necessary to lie and cheat.   *Robert Byrne*

255

It has been my experience that folks who have no vices have
very few virtues.

Abraham Lincoln (1809–1865)

256

The price of purity is purists.

Calvin Trillin

257

A bore is someone who, when you ask him how he is, tells you. *Variously ascribed*

258

Some people stay longer in an hour than others do in a month. *William Dean Howells (1837–1920)*

259

There are very few people who don't become more interesting when they stop talking.

Mary Lowry

260

The opposite of talking isn't listening. The opposite of talking is waiting. *Fran Lebowitz*

261

When the Emperor Constantine turned Christian, he banned the eating of sausage, which of course immediately created a whole army of sausage bootleggers and may explain why Al Capone always looked like a sausage.

Donald E. Westlake

262

A louse in the cabbage is better than no meat at all.

Pennsylvania Dutch proverb

263

The food in Yugoslavia is fine if you like pork tartare.

Ed Begley, Jr.

264

Eating an artichoke is like getting to know someone really well. *Willi Hastings*

265

I will not eat oysters. I want my food dead—not sick, not wounded—dead. *Woody Allen*

266

Only Irish coffee provides in a single glass all four essential food groups: alcohol, caffeine, sugar, and fat.

Alex Levine

267

Cogito ergo dim sum. *(Therefore I think these are pork buns.)* *Robert Byrne*

268

Anybody who doesn't think that the best hamburger place in the world is in his home town is a sissy.

Calvin Trillin

269

You can find your way across the country using burger joints
the way a navigator uses stars.

Charles Kuralt

270

Part of the secret of success in life is to eat what you like and
let the food fight it out inside.

Mark Twain (1835–1910)

271

We didn't starve, but we didn't eat chicken unless we were
sick, or the chicken was.

Bernard Malamud (1914–1986)

272

In Mexico we have a word for sushi: bait.

José Simon

273

Everything you see I owe to spaghetti.

Sophia Loren

274

Blow in its ear.
  Johnny Carson on the best way to thaw a frozen turkey

275

If you want to look young and thin, hang around old fat people.   *Jim Eason*

276

The cherry tomato is a marvelous invention, producing as it does a satisfactorily explosive squish when bitten.

Miss Manners (Judith Martin)

277

I prefer Hostess fruit pies to pop-up toaster tarts because they don't require so much cooking.

Carrie Snow

278

You are where you eat.

Pamela Fiori

279

No diet will remove all the fat from your body because the brain is entirely fat. Without a brain you might look good, but all you could do is run for public office.

Covert Bailey

280

I can get along with anybody . . . provided they're fat.

Susan Richman

281

Anybody who believes that the way to a man's heart is through his stomach flunked geography.

Robert Byrne

282

The waist is a terrible thing to mind.

Ziggy (Tom Wilson)

283

I have learned to spell hors d'oeuvres,
Which grates on many people's nerves.

Unknown

284

The trouble with eating Italian food is that five or six days later you're hungry again.

George Miller

285

There is no love sincerer than the love of food.

George Bernard Shaw (1856–1950)

286

Statistics show that of those who contract the habit of eating, very few survive.

Wallace Irwin (1875–1959)

287

Marriage is not merely sharing the fettucini, but sharing the burden of finding the fettucini restaurant in the first place.

Calvin Trillin

288

My wife and I tried to breakfast together, but we had to stop or our marriage would have been wrecked.

Winston Churchill (1874–1965)

289

My doctor gave me two weeks to live. I hope they're in August.

Ronnie Shakes

290

The trouble with heart disease is that the first symptom is often hard to deal with: sudden death.

Michael Phelps, M.D.

291

One of my problems is that I internalize everything. I can't express anger; I grow a tumor instead.

Woody Allen

292

A male gynecologist is like an auto mechanic who has never owned a car.

Carrie Snow

293

After a year in therapy, my psychiatrist said to me, "Maybe life isn't for everyone."

Larry Brown

294

Half of analysis is anal.

Marty Indik

295

Why should I tolerate a perfect stranger at the bedside of my mind?

Vladimir Nabokov (1899–1977) on psychoanalysis

296

People who say you're just as old as you feel are all wrong, fortunately.   *Russell Baker*

297

To reduce stress, avoid excitement. Spend more time with your spouse.   *Robert Orben*

298

Nancy Reagan has agreed to be the first artificial heart donor.   *Andrea C. Michaels*

299

Be true to your teeth or your teeth will be false to you.

Dental proverb

300
You're ugly. Not only that, you need a root canal.

James J. Garrett, D.D.S.

301
Attention to health is life's greatest hindrance.

Plato (427?–347 B.C.)

Plato was a bore.

Friedrich Nietzsche (1844–1900)

Nietzsche was stupid and abnormal.

Leo Tolstoy (1828–1910)

302

Never give a party if you will be the most interesting person there.

Mickey Friedman

303

Support wildlife. Throw a party.

Unknown

304

Cockroaches and socialites are the only things that can stay up all night and eat anything.

Herb Caen

305

Never mistake endurance for hospitality.

Unknown

306

Nothing spoils a good party like a genius.

Elsa Maxwell (1883–1963)

307

For a single woman, preparing for company means wiping the lipstick off the milk carton.

Elayne Boosler

308

In America, you can always find a party. In Russia, the party always finds you.   *Yakov Smirnoff*

309

The best thing about a cocktail party is being asked to it.

Gerald Nachman

310

There is nothing for a case of nerves like a case of beer.

Joan Goldstein

311

Reminds me of my safari in Africa. Somebody forgot the corkscrew and for several days we had to live on nothing but food and water.   *W.C. Fields (1880–1946)*

312

Sometimes too much to drink is barely enough.
                                    Mark Twain (1835–1910)

313

Like a camel, I can go without a drink for seven days—and have on several horrible occasions.

                                    Herb Caen

314

My grandmother is over eighty and still doesn't need glasses. Drinks right out of the bottle.

Henny Youngman

315

There is no law against composing music when one has no ideas whatsoever. The music of Wagner, therefore, is perfectly legal.

The National, *Paris, 1850*

316

The prelude to *Tristan and Isolde* sounded as if a bomb had fallen into a large music factory and had thrown all the notes into confusion.

The Tribune, *Berlin, 1871*

317

The prelude to *Tristan and Isolde* reminds me of the Italian painting of the martyr whose intestines are slowly being unwound from his body on a reel.

Eduard Hanslick (1825–1904), 1868

318

Wagner drives the nail into your head with swinging hammer blows.

P.A. Fiorentino (1806–1864)

319

9W.

Answer to the question: Do you spell your name with a V, Mr. Vagner?

Steve Allen

320

A gentleman is a man who can play the accordion but doesn't.   *Unknown*

321

There are some experiences in life which should not be demanded twice from any man, and one of them is listening to the Brahms *Requiem*.

George Bernard Shaw (1856–1950)

322

Classical music is music written by famous dead foreigners.

Arlene Heath

323

The main thing the public demands of a composer is that he be dead.　　　*Arthur Honegger (1892–1955)*

324

Do it big or stay in bed.　　　*Opera producer Larry Kelly*

325

Assassins!

Arturo Toscanini (1867–1957) to his orchestra

326

I only know two pieces—one is *Clair de Lune* and the other one isn't.

Victor Borge

327

Elvis Presley had nothing to do with excellence, just myth.

Marlon Brando

328
Anybody who has listened to certain kinds of music, or read certain kinds of poetry, or heard certain kinds of performances on the concertina, will admit that even suicide has its brighter aspects.

Stephen Leacock (1869–1944)

329
MTV is the lava lamp of the 1980's.

Doug Ferrari

330

When I was young we didn't have MTV; we had to take drugs and go to concerts.   *Steven Pearl*

331

Music is essentially useless, as life is.
George Santayana (1863–1952)

332

Show me a good loser and I'll show you a loser.
Unknown

333

Show me a good loser and I'll show you an idiot.
Leo Durocher

334

Try to hate your opponent. Even if you are playing your grandmother, try to beat her fifty to nothing. If she already has three, try to beat her fifty to three.
Danny McGoorty (1901–1970), billiard player

335

I probably couldn't play for me. I wouldn't like my attitude.
John Thompson, Georgetown basketball coach

336

A team should be an extension of the coach's personality.
My teams were arrogant and obnoxious.

Al McGuire, former basketball coach

337

My toughest fight was with my first wife.

Muhammad Ali

338

Hurting people is my business.

Sugar Ray Robinson

339

Football players, like prostitutes, are in the business of ruining their bodies for the pleasure of strangers.

Merle Kessler

340

I'm no different from anybody else with two arms, two legs, and forty-two-hundred hits.

Pete Rose

341

Any pitcher who throws at a batter and deliberately tries to hit him is a communist.

Alvin Dark, former baseball coach

342

The highlight of my baseball career came in Philadelphia's Connie Mack Stadium when I saw a fan fall out of the upper deck. When he got up and walked away the crowd booed.

Bob Uecker

343

One night we play like King Kong, the next night like Fay Wray.

Terry Kennedy, catcher for the San Diego Padres

344

If I ever needed a brain transplant, I'd choose a sportswriter because I'd want a brain that had never been used.

Norm Van Brocklin (1926–1983)

345

Stuffed deer heads on walls are bad enough, but it's worse when they are wearing dark glasses and have streamers and ornaments in their antlers because then you know they were enjoying themselves at a party when they were shot.

Ellen DeGeneris

346

Golf is a game with the soul of a 1956 Rotarian.

Bill Mandel

347

Golf is the most fun you can have without taking your clothes off.   *Chi Chi Rodriguez*

348

If Borg's parents hadn't liked the name, he might never have been Bjorn.   *Marty Indik*

349

The Rose Bowl is the only bowl I've ever seen that I didn't have to clean.   *Erma Bombeck*

350

How could I lose to such an idiot?
                A shout from chess grandmaster Aaron Nimzovich
                                    (1886–1935)

351

I hate all sports as rabidly as a person who likes sports hates common sense.   *H.L. Mencken (1880–1956)*

352

Running is an unnatural act, except from enemies and to the bathroom.
Unknown

353

I believe that professional wrestling is clean and everything else in the world is fixed.
Frank Deford

354

Art, like morality, consists of drawing the line somewhere.
G.K. Chesterton (1874–1936)

355

These is not art to me, all these squares and things. Real art has, you know, like a madonna in it.
Unknown (from the guest book at an exhibition of modern art)

356

I'm glad the old masters are all dead, and I only wish they had died sooner.

Mark Twain (1835–1910)

357

Give me a museum and I'll fill it.

Pablo Picasso (1881–1973)

358

Agree, for the law is costly.

William Camden (1551–1623)

359

It is better to be a mouse in a cat's mouth than a man in a lawyer's hands.

Spanish proverb

360

Two farmers each claimed to own a certain cow. While one pulled on its head and the other pulled on its tail, the cow was milked by a lawyer.

Jewish parable

361

Whatever their other contributions to our society, lawyers could be an important source of protein.

Guindon cartoon caption

362

Law school is the opposite of sex. Even when it's good it's lousy.

Unknown

363

How to win a case in court: If the law is on your side, pound on the law; if the facts are on your side, pound on the facts; if neither is on your side, pound on the table.

Unknown

364

Injustice is relatively easy to bear; what stings is justice.

H.L. Mencken (1880–1956)

365

Nobody wants justice. *Alan Dershowitz*

366

I'm not an ambulance chaser. I'm usually there before the ambulance. *Melvin Belli*

367

I never travel without my diary. One should always have something sensational to read.

Oscar Wilde (1854–1900)

368

The Irish are a fair people—they never speak well of one another. *Samuel Johnson (1709–1784)*

369

There are still parts of Wales where the only concession to gaiety is a striped shroud. *Gwyn Thomas*

370

I don't have any idea what I'm doing here. I didn't even know Alaska Airlines had a flight to Leningrad.

Bob and Ray

371

In Italy a woman can have a face like a train wreck if she's blonde.   *Unknown*

372

If you are going to America, bring food.

Fran Lebowitz

373

California is a great place to live if you're an orange.
Fred Allen (1894–1956)

374

In California you lose a point off your IQ every year.
Truman Capote (1924–1984)

375

Nothing is wrong with Southern California that a rise in the ocean level wouldn't cure.
Ross MacDonald (1915–1983)

376

There are two million interesting people in New York and only seventy-eight in Los Angeles.
Neil Simon

377

It is true that I was born in Iowa, but I can't speak for my twin sister.
Abigail Van Buren (Dear Abby)

378

Parts of Texas look like Kansas with a goiter.
Unknown

379

I have just returned from Boston. It is the only thing to do if you find yourself there.   *Fred Allen (1894–1956)*

380

Thanks to the Interstate Highway System, it is now possible to travel from coast to coast without seeing anything.

Charles Kuralt

381

One of the first things schoolchildren in Texas learn is how to compose a simple declarative sentence without the word *shit* in it.   *Unknown*

382

The town was so dull that when the tide went out it refused to come back.   *Fred Allen (1894–1956)*

383

If you don't miss a few planes during the year you are spending too much time at airports.

Paul C. Martin

384

It is now possible for a flight attendant to get a pilot pregnant.
Richard J. Ferris, president, United Airlines

385

The odds against there being a bomb on a plane are a million to one, and against two bombs a million times a million to one. Next time you fly, cut the odds and take a bomb.

Benny Hill

386

If God had intended us to fly he would never have given us railways.
Michael Flanders

387

There are two kinds of air travel in the United States, first class and third world.
Bobby Slayton

388

Thank God men cannot as yet fly and lay waste the sky as well as the earth!

Henry David Thoreau (1817–1862)

389

Art is I; science is we.

Claude Bernard (1813–1878)

390

Life is extinct on other planets because their scientists were more advanced than ours.   *Unknown*

391

A stitch in time would have confused Einstein.

Unknown

392

Great moments in science: Einstein discovers that time is actually money.

Gary Larson cartoon caption

393

Technological progress is like an axe in the hands of a pathological criminal.   *Albert Einstein (1879–1955)*

394

Technology is a way of organizing the universe so that man doesn't have to experience it.

Max Frisch

395

Horsepower was a wonderful thing when only horses had it.

Unknown

396

Men have become the tools of their tools.

Henry David Thoreau (1817–1862)

397

The computer is down. I hope it's something serious.

Stanton Delaplane

398

Rivers in the United States are so polluted that acid rain makes them cleaner. *Andrew Malcolm*

399

A two-pound turkey and a fifty-pound cranberry—that's Thanksgiving dinner at Three-Mile Island.

Johnny Carson

400

The scientific theory I like best is that the rings of Saturn are composed entirely of lost airline luggage.

Mark Russell

401

Energy experts have announced the development of a new fuel made from human brain tissue. It's called assohol.

George Carlin

402

What a beautiful fix we are in now; peace has been declared.

Napoleon Bonaparte (1769–1821) after the Treaty of Amiens, 1802

403

I thoroughly disapprove of duels. If a man should challenge me, I would take him kindly and forgivingly by the hand and lead him to a quiet place and kill him.

Mark Twain (1835–1910)

404

There is nothing more exhilarating than to be shot at without result.   *Winston Churchill (1874–1965)*

405

Nobody ever forgets where he buried the hatchet.

Kin Hubbard (1868–1930)

406

Will the last person out of the tunnel turn out the light?

Graffito in Saigon, 1973

407

We are what we are.   *Motto of Lake Wobegone, according to Garrison Keillor*

408

You gotta live somewhere.

*Motto for Cleveland
suggested by Jimmy Brogan*

409

It's a living.

Motto for the U.S. Army suggested by Mort Sahl

410

What died?

*Motto for New Jersey suggested
by Steven Pearl*

411

What the hell are you looking at?

*License plate slogan for New York suggested
by Steven Pearl*

412

Eat cheese or die.

Motto for Wisconsin suggested by Joel McNally

413

Not you.

*Bumper sticker in the state where the license plate
slogan is You've Got a Friend in Pennsylvania*

414

You appeal to a small, select group of confused people.

Message in fortune cookie

415

Ignore previous cookie.

Message in fortune cookie

416

You make God sick.

Message in fortune cookie received by Rick Reynolds

417

There is nothing wrong with Hollywood that six first-class funerals wouldn't solve.

Unknown

418

The length of a film should be directly related to the endurance of the human bladder.

Alfred Hitchcock (1899–1980)

419

A team effort is a lot of people doing what I say.

Michael Winner, British film director

420

You just gotta save Christianity, Richard! You gotta!

Loretta Young to Richard the Lionhearted in the movie The Crusades, *1935*

421

Yer beautiful in yer wrath! I shall keep you, and in responding to my passions, yer hatred will kindle into love.

John Wayne as Genghis Khan to Susan Hayward in the movie The Conqueror, *1956*

422

I've met a lot of hard-boiled eggs in my time, but you—
you're twenty minutes!

From the movie Ace in the Hole, *1951*

423

When Elizabeth Taylor meets a man she takes him and
squeezes the life out of him and then throws away the pulp.

Eddie Fisher's mother

424

Elsa Lanchester looks as though butter wouldn't melt in her
mouth, or anywhere else.

Maureen O'Hara

425

They used to photograph Shirley Temple through gauze.
They should photograph me through linoleum.

Tallulah Bankhead (1903–1968)

426

Clark Gable's ears make him look like a taxicab with the
doors open.   *Howard Hughes (1905–1976)*

427

I saw the sequel to the movie *Clones,* and you know what?
It was the same movie!

Jim Samuels

428

If you get to be a really big headliner, you have to be prepared for people throwing bottles at you in the night.

Mick Jagger

429

You have to have a talent for having talent.

Ruth Gordon (1897–1985)

430

Now that I'm over sixty I'm veering toward respectability.

Shelley Winters

431

A starlet is any woman under thirty not actively employed in a brothel.

Unknown

432

The human race is faced with a cruel choice: work or daytime television.

Unknown

433

Television is democracy at its ugliest.

Paddy Chayevsky (1923–1982)

434

Television enables you to be entertained in your home by people you wouldn't have in your home.

David Frost

435

Imitation is the sincerest form of television.

Fred Allen (1894–1956)

436

Never miss a chance to have sex or appear on television.

Gore Vidal

437

The cable TV sex channels don't expand our horizons, don't make us better people, and don't come in clearly enough.

Bill Maher

438

Babies on television never spit up on the Ultrasuede.

Erma Bombeck

439

Men and nations behave wisely once they have exhausted all the other alternatives.

Abba Eban

440

What luck for rulers that men do not think.

Adolf Hitler (1889–1945)

441

Every government is run by liars and nothing they say should be believed.

I.F. Stone

442

It is dangerous to be right when the government is wrong.
Voltaire (1694–1778)

443

Patriotism is the veneration of real estate above principles.
George Jean Nathan (1882–1958)

444

Patriotism is a pernicious, psychopathic form of idiocy.
George Bernard Shaw (1856–1950)

445

There is but one way for a newspaperman to look at a politician and that is down.
Frank H. Simonds (1878–1936)

446

Don't burn the flag; wash it.
Norman Thomas (1884–1968)

447

The reason there are so few female politicians is that it is too much trouble to put makeup on two faces.
Maureen Murphy

448

Democracy is being allowed to vote for the candidate you dislike least.
Robert Byrne

449

Diplomacy is the art of saying "Nice doggie" until you can find a rock.   *Will Rogers (1879–1935)*

450

An honest politician is one who when he is bought will stay bought.   *Simon Cameron (1799–1889)*

451

A communist is a person who publicly airs his dirty Lenin.
Jack Pomeroy

452

A conservative is a man who wants the rules changed so that no one can make a pile the way he did.

Gregory Nunn

453

Liberals feel unworthy of their possessions. Conservatives feel they deserve everything they've stolen.

Mort Sahl

454

A conservative doesn't want anything to happen for the first time; a liberal feels it should happen, but not now.

Mort Sahl

455

Conservative, n. A statesman who is enamored of existing evils, as distinguished from the liberal, who wishes to replace them with others.   *Ambrose Bierce*

456

They dug up an ancient Chinese emperor a while back who was encased in jade. I prefer gold.

Ed Koch, mayor of New York City

457

Too bad the only people who know how to run the country are busy driving cabs and cutting hair.

George Burns

458

Those who are too smart to engage in politics are punished by being governed by those who are dumber.

Plato (427?–347 B.C.)

Plato was a bore.

Friedrich Nietzsche (1844–1900)

Nietzsche was stupid and abnormal.

Leo Tolstoy (1828–1910)

459

If the Republicans will stop telling lies about the Democrats, we will stop telling the truth about them.

Adlai Stevenson (1900–1965)

460

In America, anyone can become president. That's one of the risks you take.

Adlai Stevenson (1900–1965)

461

Calvin Coolidge didn't say much, and when he did he didn't say much.

Will Rogers (1879–1935)

462

I think the American public wants a solemn ass as president. And I think I'll go along with them.

Calvin Coolidge (1872–1933)

463

He's alive but unconscious, just like Gerald Ford.

From the movie Airplane, *1980*

464

Your public servants serve you right.

Adlai Stevenson (1900–1965)

465

It's the responsibility of the media to look at the president with a microscope, but they go too far when they use a proctoscope.   *Richard M. Nixon*

466

When we got into office, the thing that surprised me the most was that things were as bad as we'd been saying they were.
                                        John F. Kennedy (1917–1963)

467

It's our fault. We should have given him better parts.
                        Jack Warner on hearing that Ronald Reagan
                        had been elected governor of California

468

I have left orders to be awakened at any time in case of national emergency, even if I'm in a cabinet meeting.
                                        Joke by Ronald Reagan,
                        current president of the United States

469

Ronald Reagan is the first president to be accompanied by a Silly Statement Repair Team.

                                        Mark Russell

470

I'm glad Reagan is president. Of course, I'm a professional comedian.   *Will Durst*

471

Reagan is proof that there is life after death.

Mort Sahl

472

There is no distinctly American criminal class—except Congress.

Mark Twain (1835–1910)

473

They should stop calling Reagan and Gorbachev the two most powerful men in the world. Between the two of them they couldn't bench press a hundred pounds.

Al Ordover

474

Gary Hart is just Jerry Brown without the fruit flies.

Robert Strauss

475

Author's Prayer:

    Our Father, which art in heaven,
    And has also written a book . . .

Unknown

476

The only reason for being a professional writer is that you can't help it.

Leo Rosten

477

In Hollywood, writers are considered only the first drafts of human beings.   *Frank Deford*

478

What an author likes to write most is his signature on the back of a check.   *Brendan Francis*

479

Very few things happen at the right time and the rest do not happen at all. The conscientious historian will correct these defects.   *Herodotus (484–425 B.C.)*

480

History will be kind to me for I intend to write it.
                                    Winston Churchill (1874–1965)

481

It is a mean thief or a successful author that plunders the dead.   *Austin O'Malley (1858–1932)*

482

The best part of the fiction in many novels is the notice that the characters are purely imaginary.
                                    Franklin P. Adams (1881–1960)

483

A detective digs around in the garbage of people's lives. A novelist invents people and then digs around in their garbage.

Joe Gores

484

Fiction is obliged to stick to possibilities. Truth isn't.

Mark Twain (1835–1910)

485

Truth is shorter than fiction.

Irving Cohen

486

The only good author is a dead author.

Book editor Patrick O'Connor

487

In six pages I can't even say "hello."

James Michener

488

Copy from one, it's plagiarism; copy from two, it's research.

Wilson Mizner (1876–1933)

489

Originality is the art of concealing your sources.

Unknown

490

There are three rules for writing a novel. Unfortunately, no one knows what they are.

W. Somerset Maugham (1874–1965)

491

Get your facts first, then you can distort them as you please.

Mark Twain (1835–1910)

492

Why don't you write books people can read?

Nora Joyce to her husband, James (1882–1941)

493

A Treasury of Filthy Religious Art Masterpieces.

Book once proposed to Simon & Schuster

494

Changing literary agents is like changing deck chairs on the
Titanic.   *Unknown*

495

You can always tell book people. They are well dressed and
their hair is really clean.

Overheard by Constance Casey
at a booksellers' convention

496

Teaching has ruined more American novelists than drink.

Gore Vidal

497

I felt like poisoning a monk.

Umberto Eco on why he wrote the novel
The Name of the Rose

498

With the single exception of Homer, there is no eminent
writer, not even Sir Walter Scott, whom I despise so entirely
as I despise Shakespeare.

George Bernard Shaw (1856–1950)

499

I feel very old sometimes . . . I carry on and would not like
to die before having emptied a few more buckets of shit on
the heads of my fellow men.

Gustave Flaubert (1821–1880)

500

To read your own poetry in public is a kind of mental incest.

Brendan Behan's father

501

Nobody ever committed suicide while reading a good book, but many have while trying to write one.

Robert Byrne

502
All newspaper editorial writers ever do is come down from the hills after the battle is over and shoot the wounded.

Unknown

503
The difference between literature and journalism is that journalism is unreadable and literature is not read.

Oscar Wilde (1854–1900)

504
Advertisements contain the only truths to be relied on in a newspaper.   *Thomas Jefferson (1743–1826)*

505
Never argue with people who buy ink by the gallon.

Tommy Lasorda

506
Some editors are failed writers, but so are most writers.

T.S. Eliot (1888–1965)

507
Every great man has his disciples, and it is always Judas who writes the biography.

Oscar Wilde (1854–1900)

508

Biography lends to death a new terror.

Oscar Wilde (1854–1900)

509

Autobiography is now as common as adultery and hardly less reprehensible.   *Lord Altrincham*

510

Autobiography is the last refuse of scoundrels.

Henry Gray

511

It's not a bad idea to get in the habit of writing down one's thoughts. It saves one having to bother anyone else with them.   *Isabel Colegate*

512

Book reviewers are little old ladies of both sexes.

John O'Hara (1905–1970)

513

Any reviewer who expresses rage and loathing for a novel is preposterous. He or she is like a person who has put on full armor and attacked a hot fudge sundae.

Kurt Vonnegut

514

People who like this sort of thing will find this the sort of thing they like.

Book review by Abraham Lincoln (1809–1865)

515

A bad review is like baking a cake with all the best ingredients and having someone sit on it.

Danielle Steel

516

Criticism is prejudice made plausible.

H.L. Mencken (1880–1956)

517

Praise and criticism arc both frauds.

Unknown

518

I am sitting in the smallest room in the house. I have your review in front of me. Soon it will be behind me.

Max Reger (1873–1916)

519

Quotations are a columnist's bullpen. Stealing someone else's words frequently spares the embarrassment of eating your own.

Peter Anderson

520

It is better to be quotable than to be honest.

Tom Stoppard

521

This isn't much of a quote book if I'm in it.

Richard Dowd, quoted here for the first time anywhere

Part III

Miscellaneous

522

There will be a rain dance Friday night, weather permitting.

George Carlin

523

Gifts are like hooks.

Martial (40?–102?)

524

Every time a friend succeeds, I die a little.

Gore Vidal

525

The goal of all inanimate objects is to resist man and ultimately defeat him.

Russell Baker

526

Cleaning anything involves making something else dirty, but anything can get dirty without something else getting clean.

Lawrence J. Peter

527

You know it's not a good wax museum when there are wicks coming out of people's heads.

Rick Reynolds

528

Everything changes but the avant garde.

Paul Valéry (1871–1945)

529

If you can't laugh at yourself, make fun of other people.

Bobby Slayton

530

The world is divided into two classes—invalids and nurses.

James McNeill Whistler (1834–1903)

531

Never mistake motion for action.

Ernest Hemingway (1889–1961)

Hemingway was a jerk.

Harold Robbins

532

I wish everybody would go back into the closet.

Josefa Heifetz

533

Some luck lies in not getting what you thought you wanted but getting what you have, which once you have got it you may be smart enough to see is what you would have wanted had you known.

Garrison Keillor

534

All God's children are not beautiful. Most of God's children are, in fact, barely presentable.

Fran Lebowitz

535

Providence protects children and idiots. I know because I
have tested it. *Mark Twain (1835–1910)*

536

The easiest kind of relationship for me is with ten thousand
people. The hardest is with one.

Joan Baez

537

Five Kids Who Make Your Kids Look Sick
  Magazine article suggested by Garrison Keillor

538

I'll not listen to reason. Reason always means what someone
else has to say.

Elizabeth Cleghorn Gaskell (1810–1865)

539

Suggested magazines:

Crotch: The International Sex Weekly

Thomas Berger

Cocker Spaniel Annual Manual

Luther Vrettos

Gimme! The Magazine of Money

Robert Byrne

The Shining (Formerly Bald World)

Robert Byrne

Beautiful Spot: A Magazine of Parking

Calvin Trillin

Poor Housekeeping (ten times the circulation of
  Good Housekeeping) *Robert Byrne*

540

Nothing is impossible for the man who doesn't have to do it himself.   *A.H. Weiler*

541

A censor is a man who knows more than he thinks you ought to.   *Granville Hicks (1901–1982)*

542

A committee is a cul-de-sac down which ideas are lured and then quietly strangled.

Sir Barnett Cocks (ca. 1907)

543

As scarce as truth is, the supply has always been in excess of the demand.   *Josh Billings (1818–1885)*

544

I never forget a face, but in your case I'll be glad to make an exception.   *Groucho Marx (1895–1977)*

545
I can mend the break of day, heal a broken heart, and provide temporary relief to nymphomaniacs.

Larry Lee

546
Hell is paved with Good Samaritans.

William M. Holden

547
Enough.
  Definition of "Once."

Ambrose Bierce (1842–1914?)

548
Anybody who thinks of going to bed before 12 o'clock is a scoundrel. *Samuel Johnson (1709–1784)*

549
A fanatic is a man who does what he thinks the Lord would do if He knew the facts of the case.

Finley Peter Dunne (1867–1936)

550
All movements go too far.

Bertrand Russell (1872–1970)

551
Never engage in a battle of wits with an unarmed person.

Unknown

552
Flies spread disease—keep yours zipped.

Unknown

553

Ya gotta do what ya gotta do.

Sylvester Stallone in the movie Rocky IV, *1985*

554

There is one thing to be said for country clubs; they drain off a lot of people you wouldn't want to associate with any-way.

Joseph Prescott

555
I do not want people to be agreeable, as it saves me the trouble of liking them.

Jane Austen (1775-1817)

556
A friend in need is a friend to dodge.

Unknown

557
Analyzing humor is like dissecting a frog. Few people are interested and the frog dies of it.

E.B. White (1899-1985)

558
A lot of people like snow. I find it to be an unnecessary freezing of water. *Carl Reiner*

559
I've only met four perfect people in my life and I didn't like any of them. *Unknown*

560
I dote on his very absence.

William Shakespeare (1564-1616)

Shakespeare is crude, immoral, vulgar, and senseless.

Leo Tolstoy (1828–1910)

561
Often it does seem a pity that Noah and his party did not miss the boat. *Mark Twain (1835–1910)*

562
You can't depend on your eyes when your imagination is out of focus. *Mark Twain (1835–1910)*

563
Only dead fish swim with the stream.

Unknown

564
I wish people wouldn't say, "Excuse me," when I *want* them to step on my feet.

Karen Elizabeth Gordon

565
Either I've been missing something or nothing has been going on. *Karen Elizabeth Gordon*

566
There are 350 varieties of shark, not counting loan and pool.

L.M. Boyd

567

When in doubt, duck.

Malcolm Forbes

568

American college students are like American colleges—each has half-dulled faculties.

James Thurber (1894–1961)

569

It took me twenty years of studied self-restraint, aided by the natural decay of my faculties, to make myself dull enough to be accepted as a serious person by the British public.

George Bernard Shaw (1856–1950)

570

The longer I live the more I see that I am never wrong about anything, and that all the pains I have so humbly taken to verify my notions have only wasted my time.

George Bernard Shaw (1856–1950)

571

I don't care what you ♥.

Bumper sticker

572

I ♠ my pets.

Bumper sticker

573

Love your enemies in case your friends turn out to be a bunch of bastards.   *R.A. Dickson*

574

One should forgive one's enemies, but not before they are hanged.   *Heinrich Heine (1797–1856)*

575

Experience teaches you to recognize a mistake when you've made it again.   *Unknown*

576

Good judgment comes from experience, and experience comes from bad judgment.

Barry LePatner

577

The trouble with using experience as a guide is that the final exam often comes first and then the lesson.

Unknown

578

It's not what we don't know that hurts, it's what we know that ain't so.   *Will Rogers (1879–1935)*

579

The world is a madhouse, so it's only right that it is patrolled by armed idiots. *Brendan Behan*

580

Consistency requires you to be as ignorant today as you were a year ago.

Bernard Berenson (1865–1959)

581

Correct me if I'm wrong, but hasn't the fine line between sanity and madness gotten finer?

George Price

582

The reason lightning doesn't strike twice in the same place is that the same place isn't there the second time.

Willie Tyler

583

The nail that sticks up gets hammered down.

Japanese proverb

584

You can lead a horse to water, but you can't make him float.

Unknown

585

If you want a place in the sun, prepare to put up with a few blisters.

Abigail Van Buren

586

I don't know, I've never been kippled.
   Answer to the question: Do you like Kipling?

Unknown

587

Ford used to have a better idea; now they don't have a clue.

Steve Kravitz

588

I can't believe that out of 100,000 sperm, you were the quickest.

Steven Pearl

589

Honesty is the best image.

Ziggy (Tom Wilson)

590

Silence is argument carried on by other means.

Ernesto "Che" Guevara (1928–1967)

591

Soderquist's Paradox:
   There are more horse's asses than horses.

From 1,001 Logical Laws, *compiled by John Peers*

592

Do Not Disturb signs should be written in the language of the hotel maids.

Tim Bedore

593

What ought to be done to the man who invented the celebrating of anniversaries? Mere killing would be too light.

Mark Twain (1835–1910)

594

Status quo. Latin for the mess we're in.

Jeve Moorman

595

Never put off until tomorrow what you can do the day after tomorrow. *Mark Twain (1835–1910)*

596

Nobody can make you feel inferior without your consent.

Eleanor Roosevelt (1884–1962)

597

An intellectual is a person whose mind watches itself.

Albert Camus (1913–1960)

598

The average person thinks he isn't.

Father Larry Lorenzoni

599

Sleep is an eight-hour peep show of infantile erotica.

J.G. Ballard

600

No man can think clearly when his fists are clenched.

George Jean Nathan (1882–1958)

601

Propaganda is the art of persuading others of what you don't believe yourself.   *Abba Eban*

602

Never believe anything until it has been officially denied.
Claud Cockburn (1904–1981)

603

There are only two ways of telling the complete truth— anonymously and posthumously.

Thomas Sowell

604

There is only one thing about which I am certain, and that is that there is very little about which one can be certain.
W. Somerset Maugham (1874–1965)

605

Before they made S. J. Perelman they broke the mold.
Unknown

606

Here's to our wives and sweethearts—may they never meet.
John Bunny (1866–1939)

607

Man Robs, Then Kills Himself.
Headline in Vancouver Province, *June 21, 1978*

608

Don't jump on a man unless he's down.

Finley Peter Dunne (1867–1936)

609

Just because your voice reaches halfway around the world doesn't mean you are wiser than when it reached only to the end of the bar.

Edward R. Murrow (1908–1965)

610

Glory is fleeting, but obscurity is forever.

Napoleon Bonaparte (1769–1821)

611

It is fun being in the same decade with you.

Franklin Delano Roosevelt (1882–1945)
in a letter to Winston Churchill, 1942

612

Although prepared for martyrdom, I preferred that it be postponed.   *Winston Churchill (1874–1965)*

613

The higher a monkey climbs, the more you see of its behind.

General Joseph "Vinegar Bend" Stilwell (1883–1946)

614

Marie Osmond makes Mother Teresa look like a slut.

Joan Rivers

615

What a strange illusion it is to suppose that beauty is goodness.
Leo Tolstoy (1828–1910)

I'm not going to climb into the ring with Tolstoy
Ernest Hemingway (1889–1961)

Hemingway was a jerk.

Harold Robbins

616

As Miss America, my goal is to bring peace to the entire world and then to get my own apartment.

Jay Leno

617

I hate the outdoors. To me the outdoors is where the car is.
Will Durst

618

The other day a dog peed on me. A bad sign.
H. L. Mencken (1880–1956)

619

He grounds the warship he walks on.

John Bracken on Captain Barney Kelly,
who ran the USS Enterprise *into the mud*
of San Francisco Bay in May of 1983

620

These are the souls that time men's tries.

Sports Illustrated *on official timers at track meets*

621

Astrology is Taurus.

F. W. Dedering

622

Nobody outside of a baby carriage or a judge's chamber believes in an unprejudiced point of view.

Lillian Hellman (1907–1984)

623

If I don't get a part for my artificial heart
I'm gonna stop caring for you.

Lyrics by Bernie Sheehan

624

I Can't Give You Anything But Love and a Baby

Song title by Willie Tyler

625

If the Phone Doesn't Ring, It's Me

Song title by Jimmy Buffet

626

It isn't that gentlemen really prefer blondes, it's just that we look dumber.

Anita Loos (1893–1981)

627

She was what we used to call a suicide blonde—dyed by her own hand.

Saul Bellow

628

For people who like peace and quiet: a phoneless cord.

Unknown

629

The best audience is intelligent, well-educated, and a little drunk.   *Alben W. Barkley (1877–1956)*

630

What is this, an audience or an oil painting?

Milton Berle

631

Civilization exists by geological consent, subject to change without notice.   *Will Durant (1885–1981)*

632

In Biblical times, a man could have as many wives as he could afford. Just like today.

Abigail Van Buren

633

The first human being who hurled an insult instead of a stone was the founder of civilization.

Attributed to Sigmund Freud (1856–1939)

634

The only paradise is paradise lost.

Marcel Proust (1871–1922)

635

Historical reminder: always put Horace before Descartes.

Donald O. Rickter

636

Most of our future lies ahead.

Denny Crum, Louisville basketball coach

637

If there is another way to skin a cat, I don't want to know about it.   *Steve Kravitz*

Sources, References, and Notes

The 637 Best Things Anybody Ever Said

The Other 637 Best Things Anybody Ever Said

The Third and Possibly The Best 637 Things
Anybody Ever Said

The 637 Best Things Anybody Ever Said

Just because this is primarily a book of humor rather than scholarship doesn't mean that credit shouldn't be given where it is due. Unfortunately, my notebooks of "Remarks Worth Remembering" and my memory are spotty on documentation, as are most of the published collections of quotations I have turned to for help. If you know an author or source I failed to give, please write to me in care of the publisher (see Introduction). With help from readers there will be fewer partial and missing ascriptions in the next edition.

I would particularly like to hear from the professional writers of comedy and gags whose handiwork is no doubt credited here and elsewhere to their celebrity clients.

The principal secondary sources I consulted are listed in

order of size, each with an identifying letter that will be referred to in the citations that follow.

A. *A New Dictionary of Quotations on Historical Principles,* Selected and edited by H. L. Mencken; Alfred A. Knopf, New York, 1952. (Approximately 37,000 entries)

B. *The Quotable Woman,* Compiled and edited by Elaine Partnow; Anchor Press/Doubleday, New York, 1978. (Approx. 21,000 entries)

C. *Familiar Quotations,* by John Bartlett; Little, Brown, Boston, 1955. (16,000 entries)

D. *The Crown Treasury of Relevant Quotations,* by Edward F. Murphy, Crown Publishers, New York, 1978. (8,000 entries)

E. *The Great Quotations,* Compiled by George Seldes; Lyle Stuart, New York, 1960. (7,000 entries)

F. *Peter's Quotations,* by Laurence J. Peter; William Morrow, New York, 1977. (6,000 entries)

G. *The Hamlyn Pocket Dictionary of Quotations,* Edited by Jonathan Hunt; The Hamlyn Publishing Group, London, 1979. (6,000 entries)

H. *The Penguin Dictionary of Modern Quotations,* J. M. and M. J. Cohen; Penguin Books, Harmondsworth, England, 1976. (5,500 entries)

I. *A Dictionary of Wit, Wisdom & Satire,* by Herbert V. Prochnow and Herbert V. Prochnow, Jr.; Harper & Row, New York, 1962. (5,000 entries)

J. *The Pocket Book of Quotations,* Edited by Henry Davidoff; Pocket Books, New York, 1952. (3,200 entries)

K. *The Book of Quotes,* by Barbara Rowes; E. P. Dutton, New York, 1979. (3,100 entries)

L. *The Quotable Quotations Book,* Compiled by Alec Lewis; Simon & Schuster, New York, 1980. (3,000 entries)

M. *The Viking Book of Aphorisms,* by W. H. Auden and Louis Kronenberger; Viking Press, New York, 1966. (3,000 entries)

N. *Popcorn in Paradise, The Wit and Wisdom of Hollywood,* Edited by John Robert Colombo; Holt, Rinehart and Winston, New York, 1980. (3,000 entries)

O. *Nobody Said It Better,* by Miriam Ringo; Rand McNally, Chicago, Ill., 1980. (2,700 entries)

P. *Proverbs and Epigrams;* Ottenheimer Publishers, Baltimore, Md., 1954. (2,500 entries)
Q. *Quotations of Wit and Wisdom,* John W. Gardner and Francesca Gardner Reese; W. W. Norton, New York, 1975. (1,200 entries)
R. *The Book of Insults,* Compiled by Nancy McPhee; St. Martin's Press, New York, 1978. (1,000 entries)
S. *The Writer's Quotation Book,* Edited by James Charlton; Pushcart Press, Yonkers, N.Y., 1980. (350 entries)

Quotation Number

1. As given in R.
2. "Selections From the Allen Notebooks," in *Without Feathers,* 1975.
5. *Sisyphus.*
6. *Twilight of the Idols,* 1889.
7. *Mackeral Plaza,* 1958.
14. *Anthony Adverse,* 1933.
17. *Soldier, Sage, Saint,* 1978.
18. *One Fat Englishman,* 1963.
19. Possibly a corruption of something Thoreau said about fishing.
21. *The San Francisco Chronicle,* July 20, 1981.
24. *A Certain Slant of Light,* 1980.
25. A "Peanuts" comic strip.
26. As given in L.
27. From a "Peanuts" comic strip, January 1982.
28. *Coop,* 1978.
29. See 270.
30. As given in I.
32. *A Book About Myself,* 1922.
33. As given in M.
34. *The Tragedy of Pudd'nhead Wilson,* 1894.
35. Quoted in *On Being Funny,* by Eric Lax. 1975.
38. *Newsweek,* June 23, 1975.
39. *Seattle Times.*
41. As given in J.
42. *Metropolitan Life,* 1978.
47. *Barrett Wendell and His Letters,* 1924.
49. *The Ginger Man,* 1965.

51. First sentence of the short story *An Imperfect Conflagration.*
52. *Death, A Poem.*
53. *Murder Considered As One of the Fine Arts,* 1827.
54. As given in A. It has been suggested that some of the quotes ascribed to Anonymous in Mencken's great work were written by Mencken himself. This could be one of them.
55. *A Day at the Races,* 1936.
58. Quoted by Anatole Broyard in a *New York Times* book review, 1980.
59. *The San Francisco Chronicle,* June 5, 1981.
60. *The Pushcart Prize V,* 1980.
65. Quoted in *Omni.*
70. *Rhetoric II.*
72. *A Glass Eye at the Keyhole,* 1938.
73–75 *The Devil's Dictionary,* 1906; all have been shortened.
82. *The Devil's Dictionary,* 1906.
83. As quoted in *The San Francisco Chronicle,* April 12, 1981.
84. As given in M.
88. *Notebooks.*
89. *You Don't Have To Be in Who's Who to Know What's What,* 1980.
90. As given in K.
95. *Nature,* 1841.
98. Quoted in *The San Francisco Chronicle,* November 11, 1979.
101. *The Rules of Christian Manners and Civility,* 1695.
105. *Conversations with Gore Vidal,* 1981.
107. As given in B.
108. *Books of the Times,* Vol. II, #7, p. 333.
110. As given in N.
111. *My Early Life,* 1930.
113. Quoted in "The Verbal Karate of Florynce Kennedy," by Gloria Steinem, *Ms.,* March 1973.
114. *Man in the Holocene,* 1980.
121. *Miss Tallulah Bankhead,* by Lee Israel, 1972.
122. *Karl Kraus,* by Harry Zohn, 1980.
124. *Reasons of the Heart,* 1965.

125. *The Most of Malcolm Muggeridge,* 1966.
126. *Vile Bodies,* 1930
129. *Soliloquies I.*
135. As given in Q.
140. As given in Q.
142. *The Picture of Dorian Gray,* 1891.
143. *Reflections of a Bachelor Girl,* 1903.
144. *The Way of All Flesh,* 1903.
147. See 82.
149. As given in A.
150. Quoted by Sara Mayfield in *The Constant Circle,* 1968.
153. Quoted by *The New York Times,* April 29, 1956.
155. The script was written by Billy Wilder and was based on the story and play by Francis Verber.
156. Quoted in *Womanlist,* by Weiser and Arbeiter, 1981.
159. Quoted in *Funny People,* by Steve Allen, 1981.
161. TS to RB.
163. From *Happy to Be Here,* 1982. Mr. Keillor uses the third person.
164. Quoted in L. M. Boyd's syndicated newspaper column, *The Grab Bag.*
168. As given in A.
170. As given in E.
174. As given in Q.
175. As given in D.
177. *Don Quixote,* 1605.
179. Sasuly is the author of *Bookies and Bettors,* 1982.
180. Quoted by RB in *McGoorty, The Story of a Billiard Bum,* 1980.
182. Quoted by Charles McCabe in *The San Francisco Chronicle,* June 30, 1978.
186. *The Decline and Fall of Practically Everybody,* 1950.
187. See 186.
188. WH to RB.
196. *Tropic of Cancer,* 1934.
197. As given in I.
198. *Maxims for Revolutionaries,* 1903.
201. *Everybody's Political What's What.*
202. SD is a San Francisco disc jockey.
204. *Legend: Tolstoy's Letters,* 1978.
205. As given in O.

210. As given in Q.
211. In an interview.
217. Quoted by Herbert Mitgang in *The New York Times Book Review*, July 1980.
218. Quoted by William Buckley in *The New York Times Book Review*, April 24, 1977.
219. *New York Times Book Review*, September 16, 1979.
222. As given in S.
223. From his *Journal*.
224. As given in E.
225. As given in E.
226. As recalled by Richard Sasuly (see 179).
230. Also ascribed to others.
238. Slightly shortened.
239. TS to RB.
243. See 42.
247. As given in A.
249. Unnamed "philosopher" quoted by Ron Butler in *San Francisco Examiner*, July 12, 1981.
250. *You Might As Well Live*.
253. *Poor Richard*, Act I, 1963.
254. Quoted in *Variety*.
255. See 150.
256. Quoted in *Reader's Digest*, November 1960.
257. According to reader Robert B. Gibson, TW used this classic spoonerism without the "free" and the "pre" on the Fernwood 2-Night television show on 9-12-77.
258. Quoted in *Life*, January 1981.
259. As given in K.
263. ARL was Teddy Roosevelt's daughter. For more see *Mrs. L: Conversations with Alice Roosevelt Longworth*, by Michael Teague, 1981.
269. Verbatim transcript, press conference.
270. Quoted by Leo Rosten in *Infinite Riches*, 1978.
271. From the White House tapes.
272. As given in K.
274. Quoted by Jack Anderson, May 1979.
278. Quoted in *Life*. January 1981.
280. In Jeff Davis's column in the *San Francisco Examiner*, October 12, 1980.

284. Quoted by Herb Caen in his *San Francisco Chronicle* column, January 28, 1981.

285. Quoted in *The Pacific Sun,* March 21, 1981.

288. See 269.

290. As given in H.

294. Quoted in *Life,* August 5, 1946.

295. From a letter quoted by Charles McCabe in his *San Francisco Chronicle* column, October 24, 1980.

297. *The Decay of Lying,* 1891.

298. Quoted by Peter De Vries in *The New York Times Book Review,* December 6, 1981.

299. As given in R.

300. *The Smart Set,* November 1920, p. 140.

301. *The Good Word,* 1978.

307. Attorney AH to RB.

311. Quoted by Herb Caen in *The San Francisco Chronicle,* June 1980. AL is the former basketball coach at the University of Texas.

314. RO is a professional gag writer who markets his work to a wide variety of celebrities and politicians, enabling them to feign wit where none exists.

315. Needlepoint sampler recalled by Debi McFarland for RB.

316. *Miss Piggy's Guide to Life,* 1981, by Henry Beard.

317. *The Picture of Dorian Gray,* 1891.

318. As given in Q.

319. *Rhetoric,* c. 322 B.C.

322. As given in K.

323. As given in K.

326. On *The Dick Cavett Show,* July 21, 1981.

327. As given in R.

336. From his *Letters.*

339. *Life on the Mississippi,* 1883.

343. CM is a *San Francisco Chronicle* columnist.

344. *Murphy's Law,* by Arthur Block, 1977.

345. *The Official Rules,* Paul Dickson, 1978.

346. *Down Shoe Lane.*

347. See 345.

348. *Journal,* February 3, 1860.

350. See 164.

361. *Brevia.*

362. As recalled by Charles Champlin.

363. *A Night at the Opera,* 1935.

364. Quoted in *The Observer,* August 28, 1949.

365. *The Goon Show,* with Peter Sellers, Spike Milligan, and others, ran on BBC radio from 1951 to 1958.

366. As given in H.

367. *The Comments of Moung Ka.*

368, 369. *The Catcher in the Rye,* 1951.

370. *Nausea,* January 1932.

372. *New York Times Magazine,* 1953.

374. *Best Sports Stories,* 1978.

378. "A Guide to Some of the Lesser Ballets," in *Without Feathers,* 1975.

379. As given in I.

381. In concert at the Hungry i in San Francisco, July 1965.

384. Ascribes to Katharine Hepburn in N.

387. As given in R.

388. *Who's Nobody in America,* by Fulwiler and Evans, 1981.

390. Reported by Herb Caen in *The San Francisco Chronicle,* April 24, 1980.

392. As given in N.

395. In various newspapers, 1978.

396. Quoted in Terence O'Flaherty's column, *The San Francisco Chronicle,* March 18, 1980.

397. Rewritten to conform to current postal rates.

404. Also said of other people.

405. *Newsweek,* March 28, 1960.

406, 407. See 263.

412. *Duck Soup,* 1933.

416. As given in N.

418. See 34.

424. *The Case of Wagner.*

425. *A View From a Broad,* 1980.

427. As given in N.

428. *Chips Off the Old Benchley,* 1949.

432. *The Constant Wife,* 1926.

433. *Our Betters,* 1923.

434. See 113.

435. *Inside Mr. Enderby,* 1968.

436. *Farewell, My Lovely,* 1940.

437. 1962.

440. In an interview with Barbara Walters.

441. JC was a writer for the *New York Post*.

443. *Unreliable Memoirs*, 1981.

444. The author probably is Paul Valéry (1871–1945) and not Arthur C. Clarke.

446. BH to RB.

447. As given in Q.

450. As recalled by Andre Previn and quoted by Herb Caen, *The San Francisco Chronicle*, February 1982.

451. The line "Forgive your enemies, but do not forget them," appears in the 1927 silent movie *Napoleon*, written and directed by Abel Gance.

453. *Finishing Touches*, Act III, 1973.

454. *Soon To Be a Major Motion Picture*, 1980.

456. As given in E.

457. Quoted in *A Thinking Man's Guide to Baseball*, 1967, by Leonard Koppet.

464. Quoted by Anatole Broyard in *The New York Times Book Review*, June 7, 1981.

465. *The Cat and the King*, 1981.

466. From an article on parental advice by Anthony Brown, distributed by *The Los Angeles Times* Syndicate.

467. *Rowing Toward Eden*, 1981.

469. As quoted by *The PG&E Progress*, January 1981.

474. Quoted by Dave Kindred in *The Washington Post*.

477. RL to RB.

478. In his syndicated newspaper column.

483. In an article on the death of *Scanlon's Magazine*, *Harper's*, April 1981.

485. In a letter to Sir Frederick Pollock.

488. In the story "Tlon, Uqbar, Orbis Tertius."

489. *The Young Immigrants*, 1920.

493. *The Medusa and the Snail*, 1979.

497. *Consenting Adults*, 1981.

504. And not his countryman, Hermann Goering.

507. See 270.

508. See 270.

509. A slightly different version appears in Herb Caen's column in *The San Francisco Chronicle*, May 1978. Mr. Wegner can be found at Trinity University in San Antonio, Texas.

512. Quoted by Merla Zellerbach in *The San Francisco Chronicle,* December 31, 1980.
515. *Dialogues in Limbo,* 1925.
516. *The Winter's Tale.*
521. *New York Times Book Review,* May 8, 1979.
523, 524. MH was a professor of Greek and Latin at Columbia.
530. *How to Prosper in the Coming Bad Years,* 1979.
534. Quoted in *Funny People,* by Steve Allen, 1981.
536. *The San Francisco Chronicle,* February 9, 1981.
538. *Household Hints,* 1966.
541. As given in M.
542. *Write If You Get Work,* 1975.
543. As given in F.
544. From a letter dated 1796.
545. *The Fall,* 1957.
546. *The Flying Inn,* 1912.
548. In a letter to Charles Green Shaw.
549. Quoted by Aldous Huxley in *Heaven and Hell,* 1956.
550. *The San Francisco Chronicle,* January 21, 1982.
551. Quoted by Herb Caen, *The San Francisco Chronicle,* February 14, 1982.
552. By Erskine & Moran, 1981.
553. As given in N.
555. Quoted in *The Wall Street Journal.*
559. *The Model Millionaire,* 1887.
560. *The Love Nest,* 1963.
561. *The Mythmakers,* 1979.
569. *Faust,* 1808.
570. *The Last Word.*
571. *Why I Am Not a Christian,* 1950.
574. *The Capitalist Handbook.*
576. From her *Letters.*
577. *The History of the French Revolution,* 1837.
579. June 26, 1979.
580. See 488.
581. Compiled from various interviews.
583. As given in K.
585. See 583.
586. *The Tonight Show,* February 7, 1979.
588. See 180.

590. From a poem titled "Put Back Those Whiskers, I Know You," in *Good Intentions,* 1942.

591. *Many Long Years Ago,* 1945.

592. Quoted by George Bernard Shaw in the preface to *Androcles and the Lion,* 1912.

593. *The House of the Seven Gables,* 1851.

598. *My Ten Years in a Quandary,* 1936.

599. See 598.

600. Quoted by Leacock in *Humor: Its Theory and Technique,* 1935.

601. *Too Much College,* 1941.

602. "Gertrude the Governess," in *Nonsense Novels,* 1914.

605. As given in F.

606. As given in F.

607. "Selections From the Allen Notebooks," in *Without Feathers,* 1975.

609. *Versus,* 1949.

611. JH to RB about a television talk-show host, 1970.

612. As given in K.

613. See 140.

614. See 34.

615. *Polite Conversation,* 1738.

619. *New York Times Book Review.*

620. As given in B.

622. Before his retirement in 1981, KHA was in charge of the San Francisco Opera Company.

624. *Dialogues,* 1954.

626. As given in F.

628. To C. A. Dana, April 1865.

629. *Euphues,* 1579.

633. As quoted by Allison Silver in *The New York Times Book Review,* February 28, 1982.

636. As given in K.

The Other 637 Best Things Anybody Ever Said

Like other books of quotations, this one owes a heavy debt to anthologists who have gone before. The principal secondary sources I used in supplementing my own reading and eavesdropping are listed below and referred to in the citations by the letters assigned to them.

Readers who point out misquotations or supply missing sources will be thanked in future printings, if any. Favorite lines (nothing pompous, please) also will be gratefully received.

Collecting quotations is an insidious, even embarrassing habit, like ragpicking or hoarding rocks or trying on other people's laundry. I got into it originally while trying to break an addiction to candy. I kicked candy and now seem to be stuck with quotations, which are attacking my brain instead of my teeth. While I have no plans to compile a third sampler, I can't promise I won't, either.

A. H. L. Mencken, ed., *A New Dictionary of Quotations on Historical Principles* (New York: Alfred A. Knopf, 1952).
B. Jonathon Green, comp., *Morrow's International Dictionary of Contemporary Quotations* (New York: William Morrow and Company, 1982).
C. J. M. and M. J. Cohen, *The Penguin Dictionary of Modern Quotations,* 2nd ed. (Harmondsworth, England, and New York: Penguin Books, 1980).
D. John Gross, comp., *The Oxford Book of Aphorisms* (Oxford, England: Oxford University Press, 1983.)
E. Gerald F. Lieberman, *3,500 Good Quotes for Speakers* (New York: Doubleday & Company, 1983).
F. Bob Chieger, *Was It Good for You, Too? Quotations on Love and Sex* (New York: Atheneum Publishers, 1983).
G. Jonathon Green, comp., *The Book of Political Quotes* (New York: McGraw-Hill Book Company, 1982).
H. Joe Franklin, *Joe Franklin's Encyclopedia of Comedians* (Secaucus, N.J.: Citadel Press, 1979).
I. Steve Allen, *More Funny People* (New York: Stein and Day, 1982).

Quotation Number
2. As given in D.
3. *Notebooks,* 1912.
4. As given in C.

5. Quoted in the *New York Times Book Review,* October 30, 1933.
8. Linda Festa to RB.
9. As given in *Peter's Quotations* (New York: William Morrow and Company, 1977).
10. "The Tonight Show," September 31, 1982.
12. As given in D.
14. "The Tonight Show," August 11, 1982.
15. Thanks to Ms. Christopher B. Eubanks.
16. As given in E.
18. Thanks to Robert Machuta.
19. As given in F.
20. As given in D.
22. From *The Ladies Guide* (Battle Creek, Mich.: Modern Medicine Publishing Company, 1895). Dr. Kellogg helped invent cornflakes and peanut butter. In addition to denouncing masturbation, he believed that smoking caused cancer and that certain ailments could be cured by rolling a cannonball on the stomach.
23. As quoted by John Molloy in a San Francisco lecture in 1982.
24. A slightly different version is in E.
27. From the movie *Sleeper.*
28. As given in *Quotations for Writers and Speakers,* by A. Andrews.
29. As given in B.
32. Thanks to George Dushek.
35. As given in *Wihelm Meisters Lehrjahre,* 1795.
37. As given in A.
38. Linda Festa to RB.
39. Quoted in the *San Francisco Chronicle,* August 14, 1982.
40. As given in Walter Wagner, *You Must Remember This.*
41. As given in F.
42. At Cobb's Pub, San Francisco, February 3, 1984.
43. During the San Francisco Standup Comedy Competition, 1983.
44. From the movie *Everything You Wanted to Know About Sex.*
45. As given in *The Sayings of Quentin Crisp.*
47. As given in B.

48. As given in Charlotte Chandler, *The Ultimate Seduction.*
49. As given in Joseph Weintraub, ed., *The Wit and Wisdom of Mae West.*
50. As given in E.
51, 52. As given in C.
57. Thanks to Arlene Heath.
59. As given in *Who Do You Think You Are?*
61. As given in *The Well-Tempered Sentence* (New York: Ticknor & Fields).
65. As given in H.
68. As given in F.·
71. Don Rose is a San Francisco disk jockey.
72. Thanks to Arlene Heath.
73. Martin Cruz Smith to RB in jest.
76. As given in E.
78. As given in B.
79. Jim Samuels won the 1982 San Francisco Standup Comedy Competition.
80. *Newsweek,* 1980
82. As given in B.
84. As given in *Comment.*
85. As given in F.
92. As quoted by Merla Zellerbach in the *San Francisco Chronicle,* December 21, 1982.
93. Thanks to Charles DeShong.
94. As given in *The Young Duke,* 1831.
96. Interview in the *Washington Post,* January 1983.
99, 100. As given in F.
101. From the movie *Manhattan.*
103. As given in *The Watched Pot.*
106. As given in *One Fat Englishman.*
107. As given in H.
109, 110. As given in A.
111. As given in Newbern and Rodebaugh, *Proverbs of the World.*
112. As given in *Vital Parts.* Thanks to Gerald Howard.
113, 114. As given in E.
115. As given in *The British Museum Is Falling Down.*
116. As given in *The Lonely Life.*
118. Robert Orben is a professional joke writer who publishes a newsletter called *Orben's Current Comedy* that

is airmailed to subscribers. This is from the November 2, 1983, edition. The address is 700 Orange Street, Wilmington, Delaware 19801.

119. As given in E.

120. As given in *Last Words,* 1933.

123. As given in *The Measure of My Days,* 1972.

125. As given in *Newsweek,* 1978.

126. As given in B.

128. As given in Frank Muir, *The Frank Muir Book.*

129. As given in *The Old Woman.*

130. As recalled by Arlene Heath.

131. As given in *Time,* December 28, 1970.

133. As given in *Living It Up.*

134. As given in *Reginald in Russia,* 1910.

135. From the movie *Annie Hall.*

138. Thanks to Cyra McFadden.

139. Quoted by Georgia Hesse in the *San Francisco Chronicle.* Hesse added that Dom Pérignon was blind at the time.

144. As given in Herb Caen's *San Francisco Chronicle* column, November 24, 1983.

145. As given in B.

147, 148. As given in H.

149. As given in Gary Herman, comp., *The Book of Hollywood Quotes* (London: Omnibus Press, 1979). Thanks to Chris Arnold.

150. Quoted by Jimmy Breslin in his syndicated column, April 1983.

151. As given in B.

153. From *Rhinoceros,* Act II.

154. Bill Musselman is a basketball coach.

157. From the movie *Sleeper.*

160. As given in the *Observer,* April 19, 1957.

161. From *Death of a Salesman.*

162. From Larry Gelbart's introduction to I.

163. As given in *Funny, but Not Vulgar,* 1944.

164, 165. From Mordecai Richler's introduction to *The Best of Modern Humor* (New York: Alfred A. Knopf, 1983).

167. As given in Calvin Trillin's San Francisco lecture, January 18, 1984.

168. From a cable TV special called "Homage to Steve," 1984.

171. As given in *Sisterhood Is Powerful.*
174. As given in B.
175. As given in E.
176. As given in *Metropolitan Life.*
177. As given in E.
178. As given in *Kiss and Tell.*
179. As given in *Quote and Unquote.*
180. As given in B.
184. As given in *Esquire,* 1970.
184. See note 151.
189. See note 92.
190. As given in *The Saturday Evening Post,* 1952
191. A slightly different version is given in F.
193. As given in *MS* (November 1983).
194. As given in the movie *The Culture of Narcissism* (1979).
195. As given in *I'm No Angel.*
196. From Gerald Nachman's column in the *San Francisco Chronicle,* August 1982.
197. As given in B.
201. As given in *The Big Book of Jewish Humor.*
202. From the movie *My Favorite Year.*
203. As given by S. M. Ulam, *Adventures of a Mathematician* (New York: Charles Scribner's Sons, 1976).
207. As given in *The Conquest of Happiness.*
210. As given in B.
218. As given in *Jackie Mason's America* (Lyle Stuart, Inc., 1983).
219. As given in *The Painted Lady.*
220. Thanks to Linda Festa.
222. As given in *Careers for Women.*
227. See note 92.
232. Quoted by Herb Caen in the *San Francisco Chronicle,* May 17, 1983.
233. *New Yorker,* January 2, 1984.
234. As given in E.
235. As given in the *Village Voice,* April 1983.
238. As given in G.
240. As given in Joseph Heller, *Catch-22.*
242. As given in E.
243. As given in G.
244. From Will Rogers, *Autobiography.*

247. From *The Tonight Show*, February 8, 1984.
248. At The Punch Line, San Francisco, January 1984.
249. Herb Caen's column, *San Francisco Chronicle*, August 19, 1983.
251. From an article in *The San Francisco Paper*, February 1984.
252. As given in D.
253. As given in J. Green, *The Book of Rock Quotes*.
257. As given in A.
259. See note 218.
265. See note 218.
267. As given in *Orben's Current Comedy*, October 19, 1983.
268. See note 92.
272. Recalled by Calvin Trillin.
274. Thanks to Arlene Heath.
275. As given in B.
276. As given in H.
278. Steve Allen says S.B. wrote the line for him.
279. Quoted by Paul Burka in *Esquire* (April 1983).
280. As given in Andy Rooney, *And More by Andy Rooney*.
281. See note 92.
283. *The Tonight Show*, September 26, 1983.
284. Gerald Nachman is a columnist for the *San Francisco Chronicle*.
285. As given in *The Hole*.
286. Quoted by Sir Laurence Olivier on the BBC.
290. See note 92.
292, 293. See note 167.
294. As given in B.
296. As given in Herb Caen's column, *San Francisco Chronicle*, December 2, 1982.
297. As given in *The Letters of Edna St. Vincent Millay*.
298. As given in *The Men's Club*.
299. Quoted by Richard Condon in *Prizzi's Honor*.
303. Quoted by Paul Fussell in *Class*.
304. See note 92.
305. As given in D.
306. As given in the *Observer*, April 20, 1958.
307. As given in C.
310. As given in G.
311. *The Third Man* was written by Graham Greene.

313. From the TV show "Late Night with David Letterman," January 6, 1984.

314. From his nightly commentary on Channel 4 (NBC), San Francisco, September 28, 1982.

315. From her San Francisco lecture, November 4, 1983.

316. From "Late Night with David Letterman," February 9, 1984.

317. From a letter to Goodman Ace.

320. Will Durst won the 1983 San Francisco Standup Comedy Competition.

322. See note 248.

324. "The Tonight Show," September 14, 1983.

327. As given in H.

328. As given in D.

333. As given in E.

337. As given in D.

342. Thanks to Tom Stewart.

349. As given in *The Critic as Artist,* 1891.

350. Written for a competition among the paper's sub-editors for "the world's most boring headline." Described by Claud Cockburn in his *Autobiography.*

351. Cecilia Bartholomew writes and teaches writing in the San Francisco area.

352. Quoted by George Will in his syndicated column, December 20, 1983.

353. In the *New York Times Book Review,* January 1, 1984.

355. As given in B.

360. As given in *The Nature and Aim of Fiction.* Thanks to Gerald Howard.

363. As given in the *New York Times Book Review,* June 6, 1982.

364. *Afterthoughts,* 1931.

365. As given in the *Observer,* October 14, 1951.

367. As given in the *Guardian,* March 21, 1973.

369. As given in F. Scott Fitzgerald, *The Last Tycoon.*

371. As given in the *Sunday Times* (London), October 16, 1977.

372. As given in *Time,* 1957.

373. Quoted by W. H. Auden in *A Certain World.*

378, 379, 380. See note 151.

381. As given in the *New York Times Book Review,* 1971.

382. As given in the *Observer,* October 8, 1961.
383. As given in H.
398. From the movie *All About Eve,* 1950.
400. As given in *San Francisco Chronicle,* December 21, 1982.
401. As given in *San Francisco Chronicle,* January 2, 1983.
402. Arthur Gingold wrote *Items from Our Catalog.*
403. Quoted by Gerald Nachman in the *San Francisco Chronicle,* September 22, 1983.
404. Quoted by Gerald Nachman in the *San Francisco Chronicle,* July 18, 1983.
405. Quoted by Gerald Nachman in the *San Francisco Chronicle,* December 21, 1983.
407. As given in the *New York Times Magazine,* January 9, 1966.
408. As given in B.
412. As given in E.
413. Martin Cruz Smith to RB.
415. As given in F.
416. As given in C.
419. Thanks to Maureen Connolly.
427. See note 79.
429. From a Hallmark card.
435. As given in *A Madman's Diary.*
436. As given in *More in Anger,* 1958.
437. Inge was dean of St. Paul's.
438. See note 79.
439. From the radio show *The Prairie Home Companion,* June 1983.
442. As given in *Cat Scan* (New York: Atheneum, 1983).
444. Thanks to Leslie Sheridan.
446. As given in *The Diary of Alice James.*
448. As given in I.
449. As given in E.
450. As given in *Jeeves and the Hard-boiled Egg.*
452. Quoted by Harry Zohn, *Karl Kraus.*
453. As given in the *Observer,* July 19, 1975.
455. "The Tonight Show," February 10, 1984.
456. As given in the *Atlantic Monthly,* 1981.
459. As given in A. Schlesinger, Jr., *A Thousand Days.*
460, 461. As given in G.

462. As given in H.
464. As given in B.
467. "The Tonight Show," November 17, 1982.
470. See note 315.
479. Thanks to Charles T. DeShong.
485. As given in *The Book of Laughter and Forgetting*.
487. Thanks to Dick Werthimer.
488. Thanks to Robert Machuta.
490. Thanks to Charles T. DeShong.
491. Darrin Weinberg to RB.
493. See note 248.
495. John Rostoni to Teressa Skelton to RB.
499. Often called Sturgeon's Law.
500. *Improvisation.*
503. See note 61.
504. As given in *The Naked Civil Servant.*
507. As given in D.
508. As given in *Psychology in the Wry.*
514. Don Quisenberry is a baseball pitcher.
517. Teressa Skelton to RB.
518. Thanks to Bob Hudson.
520. See note 92.
521. Quoted by Herb Caen in the *San Francisco Chronicle,* May 22, 1983.
523. As given in *Orben's Current Comedy,* September 21, 1983. See note 118.
525. As given in I.
526. As given in *My Saber is Bent,* 1983. See note 118.
530. As given in *The Bald Twit Lion.*
532. As given in *Epistles.*
543. As given in *How to Become a Virgin.*
545. As given in *They and I.*
550. As given in *Present Laughter,* Act I.
552. As given in *Orben's Current Comedy,* November 17, 1983. See note 118.
556. As given in G.
557. See slightly different wording in D.
558. As given in C.
559. As given in I.
563. As given in the *Wall Street Journal,* 1975.

565. See note 151.
570. *Maxims,* 1665.
572. As given in George Robey, *Looking Back on Life.*
573. "The Tonight Show," September 14, 1983.
577. As given in *Unkempt Thoughts.*
581. As given in *Night Thought Book,* 1834.
586. Linda Festa to RB.
590. As given in *Ugly Trades.*
592. Jerry Bundsen is a former aide to Herb Caen, who quoted this line in his column in the *San Francisco Chronicle* in October 1983.
594. As given in H.
596. In the introduction to *Mother Night.*
597. As given in *Class.*
599. As given in I.
602. Quoted in the magazine *Friendly Exchange* (Winter 1982).
605. As given in *The Densa Quiz.*
606. As given in the *Observer,* 1974.
607. Thanks to Arlene Heath.
609. See note 151.
611. As given in *Social Studies.*
612, 613. As given in B.
615. Thanks to George Dushek.
618. As given in F.
622. As given in *Quality Street,* Act III.
623. As given in William Fifield, *In Search of Genius.*
624. As given in *The Devil's Dictionary.*
625. As given in *Poor Richard's Almanac.*
626. As given in *Speedboat.* Thanks to Gerald Howard.
629. Thanks to George Dushek.
631. As given in *On Reading and Books,* 1851.
634. As given in letter to T. J. Hogg, 1821.
635. As given in Stanton Delaplane's column in the *San Francisco Chronicle,* March 7, 1934.
636. "The Tonight Show," March 13, 1984.

The Third and Possibly the Best 637 Best Things Anybody Ever Said

Quotations are indexed here only when I have something useful to add. Readers with corrections or who can supply missing information are urged to write to me in care of Fawcett Books, 201 E. 50th Street, New York, New York 10022.

Quotation Number

2. BS in a letter to RB.
3. JDM in the *Bulletin,* 1974
5. LT in *What Is Religion?,* 1902.
8. HLM in an Associated Press interview, 1941.
9. RM in *The Towers of Trebizond,* 1956.
10. Quoted by G. M. Thomson in *Vote of Censure,* 1968.
11. BM in a speech in Lausanne, 1904.
13. CK is a standup comedian.
14. SR wrote the line for the character Archie Bunker in the third episode of All in the Family.
16. Quoted in the *San Francisco Chronicle,* December 17, 1985.
17. According to William Safire in his syndicated column, December 8, 1985.
18. FN in *Thus Spake Zarathustra.*
19. EH in a letter.
20. HR as quoted in Leslie Halliwell's *The Filmgoer's Companion,* 1984.
22. RS is a standup comedian.
25. From *The Cynic's Lexicon,* compiled by Jonathon Green, 1982.
26. Thanks to David Huard.
27. FN in *Thus Spake Zarathustra,* 1891.
28. Quoted in *3500 Good Quotes for Speakers,* compiled by Gerald F. Lieberman, 1983.
30. NW quoted in *Was It Good for You, Too?* compiled by Bob Chieger, 1983.
31. WA in *Play It Again, Sam,* 1969.
33. Quoted in the *San Francisco Sunday Chronicle-Examiner,* September 1, 1985.

35. O in *Ars Amatoria.*
36. J in *Satires,* A.D. 110.
37. From *A New Dictionary of Quotations on Historical Principles,* compiled by H. L. Mencken, 1952.
39. SR in the *San Francisco Chronicle,* August 2, 1985.
44. Taken from the jacket of MP's 1985 book *Shoes Never Lie.*
45. AC is a standup comedian.
47. Quoted in the comedy trade paper *Just for Laughs,* August 1985.
51. Quoted in *Forbes,* September 16, 1985.
53. JM in *Miss Manners' Guide to Excruciatingly Correct Behavior,* 1985.
54. JV is a standup comedian.
55. MD in *Dogs Are Better Than Cats,* 1985.
56. RB in the *Atlantic Monthly,* February 1985.
57. EB is a standup comedian.
58. MP is a standup comedian.
62. Quoted in the *San Francisco Chronicle,* December 31, 1984.
63. "The Tonight Show," January 10, 1985.
64. RO in *Orben's Current Comedy,* a weekly newsletter of topical gags, November 6, 1985.
65. JM in *Common Courtesy,* 1985.
66. ARC was interviewed by the *New York Times* in December 1985. He was quoted further as saying that he didn't rule out the possibility that the honor bestowed on him was a political smear.
68. See note 37.
70. Quoted by HG in his autobiographical novel *Family.*
72. Thanks to H. Peter Metzger.
73. From *Miss Piggy's Guide to Life,* 1981, as told to HB.
74. From *Quote,* November 1, 1985.
75. MS to RB.
76. From the Peanuts comic strip, April 1984.
78. KW is a popular columnist in Great Britain.
80. GK on his radio show "A Prairie Home Companion," July 21, 1985.
83. AH in the *San Francisco Chronicle,* November 25, 1985.
84. Quoted in *The Cynic's Lexicon,* compiled by Jonathon Green, 1982.

85. AC in the *New York Times,* February 18, 1968.
86. MW at the San Francisco Standup Comedy Competition, 1979.
88. GG in a letter to the *Journal of Irreproducible Results.*
89. RY in *Family Weekly,* 1977.
92. Thanks to Marty Indik.
95. GS is a standup comedian.
97. GS on "The Tonight Show," August 17, 1985.
98. Seen in London by Herb Caen.
99. WD won the 1983 San Francisco Standup Comedy Competition.
100. Given in *Was It Good for You, Too?* compiled by Bob Chieger, 1983.
101. JK is a standup comedian.
104. MM is a standup comedian.
105. Quoted by Peter Stack in the *San Francisco Chronicle,* October 4, 1985. RL is a standup comedian.
106. GL is publisher of *High Society.*
107. AB in *Rolling Stone,* July 14, 1977.
112. PD in his 1955 novel *Major Thompson Lives in France and Discovers the French.*
114. LB in *Don Juan,* 1819.
116. BN is a standup comedian. Thanks to Pete Harley.
117. Thanks to Lee Simon.
118. GS is a standup comedian.
119. WT is a standup comedian.
121. MD to RB.
124. From the movie *She Done Him Wrong* (1933), screenplay by MW.
129. MS in the *New York Times Book Review,* November 6, 1985.
132. GN is a columnist and critic for the *San Francisco Chronicle.*
134. *Out of Africa,* screenplay by Kurt Luedtke based on books by and about Isak Dinesen.
135. SB in *Men: An Owner's Manual,* 1984.
136. CS is a standup comedian.
138. GN in the *San Francisco Chronicle,* February 26, 1985.
139. GK in his San Francisco lecture, December 13, 1984.
141. Thanks to Susan Richman.
142. Thanks to Arlene Heath.

143. RM in *The Towers of Trebizond,* 1956.
145. Quoted in *Was It Good for You, Too?* compiled by Bob Chieger, 1983.
147. Thanks to Merla Zellerbach.
149. Thanks to Susan Richman.
150. Quoted by Herb Caen in the *San Francisco Chronicle,* December 23, 1983.
151. DS on "The Tonight Show," 1972.
156. See note 64.
158. PP is a standup comedian.
159. See note 64.
161. SP is a standup comedian.
165. In *Letter and Journals* (New York: Viking, 1985).
166. LPS in *Afterthoughts,* 1934.
167. EP is a standup comedian.
174. WS is a standup comedian.
175. MS to RB.
180. LH on "Freeman Reports," November 30, 1985.
181. Thanks to Joe Gores.
184. In RB's biography *McGoorty,* 1972 and 1984.
186. JG in *Esquire,* April 1983.
187. Thanks to Knox Burger.
191. LPS in *All Trivia,* 1949.
193. See note 64.
194. RM at a San Francisco press conference, May 21, 1985.
199. Quoted by Merla Zellerbach in the *San Francisco Chronicle,* March 7, 1984.
200. Quoted in the *Little Dublin News,* March 1985, published in Dubuque, Iowa.
208. LB in the *San Francisco Examiner,* July 15, 1984.
220. HC in the *San Francisco Chronicle,* April 28, 1985.
226. FML to RB.
228. GK in his San Francisco lecture, December 13, 1984.
231. JC on "The Tonight Show," November 20, 1984.
232. HC in the *San Francisco Chronicle,* December 11, 1985.
234–235. RB in his syndicated *New York Times* column, September 22, 1985.
236. DTW to RB.
238. LT in her one-woman Broadway show, 1985.
239. HAS in *Let the Crabgrass Grow,* 1960.
241. GC in *The Widow's Tears,* 1612.

242. RS is a standup comedian.
245. CK won the Pulitzer Prize for poetry in 1985.
246. Quoted in *Hot News,* published periodically by Lyle Stuart.
251. Thanks to David Huard.
252. Thanks to Marty Indik.
253. BS in *What Makes Sammy Run?* 1941.
256. CT in *American Fried,* 1979.
259. ML in the *Pacific Sun,* November 15, 1985.
260. FL in *Social Studies,* 1981.
261. DEW in *A Likely Story,* 1984.
262. EB on "The Tonight Show," September 25, 1985.
264. Quoted by Herb Caen in the *San Francisco Chronicle,* May 6, 1985.
265. WA in *Please Don't Drink the Water,* 1967.
266. Quoted by Herb Caen in the *San Francisco Chronicle,* December 13, 1984.
268. CT in *American Fried,* 1979.
271. BM in *Idiots First,* 1963.
272. JS is a standup comedian.
275. JE is a San Francisco radio talk-show host.
277. CS is a standup comedian.
279. CB in his San Rafael, California lecture, February 1985.
283. Thanks to H. Peter Metzger.
284. GM is a standup comedian.
289. RS is a standup comedian.
290. MP on the BBC World Service.
292 – 293. Delivered on Comedy Celebration Day, July 20, 1985, when sixty standup comedians performed for a total of seven hours in San Francisco's Golden Gate Park.
296. RB in his syndicated *New York Times* column, August 27, 1985.
297. See note 64.
298. Quoted by Herb Caen in the *San Francisco Chronicle,* March 7, 1985.
299. Thanks to Dr. Stephen F. Goodman.
300. JJG to RB in jest; RB didn't need a root canal.
302. Thanks to Collin Wilcox.
305. Thanks to Audrey Stanley, KARN, Little Rock.
307. EB is a standup comedian.

308. YS is a Soviet comedian who emigrated to the United States in 1981. He also said that in the United States you watch television, but in Russia television watches you.

309. GN in the *San Francisco Chronicle,* August 27, 1985.

313. HC in the *San Francisco Chronicle,* December 29, 1985. The quote is out of context, for it appeared in a column in which HC argued that drunk jokes aren't really funny and vowed to use fewer of them in his widely-read column.

315 – 318. Many quotes of this sort can be found in *The Lexicon of Musical Invective,* compiled by Nicolas Slonimsky, 1969.

319. From the Question Man segment of the old "Steve Allen Show."

320. Thanks to Kitty Sprague.

322. AH to RB.

327. MB in *Playboy,* 1979.

328. SL in *The Mariposa Bank Mystery,* 1912.

330. SP is a standup comedian.

331. GS in *The Life of Reason,* 1954.

332. Thanks to Leonard Tong.

333. As quoted by RB in *McGoorty,* 1972 and 1984.

337. Quoted by Bob Green in *Cheeseburgers.* Thanks to Tom Winston.

338. RR to the New York State Boxing Commission, May 23, 1962.

339. Quoted by Patricia Holt in the *San Francisco Chronicle,* November 13, 1985.

341. Thanks to Marty Indik.

342. BU on "Larry King Live," September 17, 1985.

345. EG is a standup comedian.

346. BD in the *San Francisco Examiner,* February 10, 1985.

349. EB was the grand marshal of the 1986 Rose Bowl Parade.

353. FD on Cable News Network, November 4, 1985.

357. Quoted by Barnaby Conrad III in the *San Francisco Chronicle,* November 24, 1985.

362–363. Thanks to Arlene Heath.

366. Quoted in the *San Francisco Chronicle,* August 10, 1985.

369. GT in *Punch,* June 18, 1958.

370. From a sketch titled *Fern Ock Veek, Sickly Whale Oil*

Processor, reprinted in *The New! Improved! Bob and Ray Book,* 1985.

371. Quoted by Stephanie von Buchau in the *Pacific Sun,* February 8, 1985.

372. FL in *Social Studies,* 1981.

373. From *Conversations with Capote,* by Lawrence Grobel.

375. RM in *The Drowning Pool,* 1951.

376. NS in *Playboy,* February 1979.

377. Letter to RB.

379. Letter to Groucho Marx, June 12, 1983.

383. Thanks to Susan Richman.

386. MF in the *New York Times,* April 16, 1975.

387. BS is a standup comedian.

388. HDT in *Journal,* January 3, 1861.

391. From *The Journal of Irreproducible Results.* Thanks to D. O. Rickter.

397. SD in the *San Francisco Chronicle,* July 11, 1984.

398. AM is the author of *The Canadians,* 1985.

399. JC on "The Tonight Show," November 20, 1984.

404. Thanks to Gary Muldoon.

406. Thanks to Harry Roach.

410. SP is a standup comedian.

412. Quoted by Leah Garchik in the *San Francisco Chronicle,* December 6, 1985.

420 – 421. Quoted in *The Hollywood Hall of Shame* by Harry and Michael Medved, 1984.

422. Screenplay by Billy Wilder, Lesser Samuels, and Walter Newman.

423. Quoted in *The Jewish Mother's Hall of Fame,* by Fred Bernstein, 1986.

428. Thanks to Marty Indik.

430. SW on "The Tonight Show," February 28, 1985.

437. BM is a standup comedian.

442. Wording by RB.

451. JP in a letter to RB.

455. AB in *The Devil's Dictionary.*

456. EK at the opening of an exhibition of jade in January 1985.

462. CC to Ethel Barrymore, according to *Time,* March 6, 1955.

463. Screenplay by Jim Abrahams and Jim and Jerry Zucker.

464. Thanks to Tom Stewart.
465. RN during an interview on CBS in 1984.
470. See note 99.
473. Al Ordover is a close personal friend of Knox Burger.
474. RS is former chairman of the Democratic party.
477. FD in *Sports Illustrated*, July 9, 1984.
478. From *The Cynic's Lexicon*, compiled by Jonathon Green, 1982.
480. Quoted by Richard Nixon to Barbara Walters, May 8, 1985.
487. JM in the introduction to Hemingway's *The Most Dangerous Summer*, 1985.
495. CC is book editor of the *San Jose Mercury-News*.
496. GV in *Oui*, April 1975.
499. GF in a letter to Ivan Turgenev, November 8, 1879.
500. Quoted by Shay Duffrin in his one-man show *Confessions of an Irish Rebel*, 1984.
504. TJ in a letter, 1819.
505. TL is the coach of the Los Angeles Dodgers.
507. OW in *The Critic as Artist*, 1890.
509. LA in the *Sunday Times*, London, February 28, 1962.
511. IC in her 1981 novel *The Shooting Party*.
513. Quoted by Thomas Fleming in the *New York Times Book Review*, January 6, 1985.
514. Thanks to Hugh Parker.
515. Quoted by Merla Zellerbach in the *San Francisco Chronicle*, December 21, 1982.
518. Quoted in *New York* magazine, July 8, 1974.
519. PA reviewing *The Other 637 Best Things Anybody Ever Said* in the *San Rafael Independent Journal*, March 21, 1985.
521. RD is chiefly known as the former roommate of Marty Indik, who himself is not particularly well known.
524. GV in the *New York Times*, February 4, 1973.
525. RB in the *New York Times*, June 18, 1968.
527. RR in the *San Francisco Examiner*, July 1, 1984.
531. Thanks to Harry Roach.
532. JH as quoted in the *Pacific Sun*, November 28, 1985.
533. GK in *Lake Wobegone Days*, 1985.
534. FL in *Metropolitan Life*, 1978.

540. AHW in the *New York Times,* 1968.
542. From *The Cynic's Lexicon,* compiled by Jonathon Green, 1982.
543. JB in *Affurisms,* 1869.
545. Thanks to Lee Simon.
546. WMH in a letter to RB.
552. Quoted by Rob Morse in the *San Francisco Examiner,* January 5, 1986.
554. JP in *Aphorisms,* privately printed in 1985.
556. Thanks to Arlene Heath.
558. Thanks to Marty Indik.
560. WS in *The Merchant of Venice.*
565. KEG in *The Well-Tempered Sentence,* 1984.
566. LMB in his syndicated column, May 5, 1985.
568. Thanks to David L. Huard.
569. GBS as quoted by Ulick O'Connor in *All the Olympians,* 1984.
570. GBS in a letter to H. G. Wells.
573. Quoted by Herb Caen in the *San Francisco Chronicle,* November 17, 1985.
577. Thanks to Robert Gordon.
579. BB as quoted by Shay Duffrin in his one-man show *Confessions of an Irish Rebel.*
581. Cartoon caption in the *New Yorker,* January 6, 1986.
582. WT is a professional ventriloquist.
584. Thanks to Jim Eason.
586. Steve Allen remembers this line from the 1930's. Letter to RB.
587. SK is a standup comedian.
588. SP is a standup comedian.
590. Thanks to Marty Indik.
594. As given in *The Dictionary of Humorous Economics.*
597. AC in *Notebooks,* 1965.
598. Quoted by Herb Caen in the *San Francisco Chronicle,* February 2, 1985.
601. AE as quoted in *The Book of Political Quotes,* compiled by Jonathon Green, 1982.
606. JB as quoted by Joe Franklin in his *Encyclopedia of Comedy,* 1979.
609. ERM as quoted by Harry Reasoner.

613. JS as quoted in *The Book of Political Quotes,* compiled by Jonathon Green, 1982.

616. JL is a standup comedian.

617. See note 99.

618. HLM in a letter. Thanks to Marty Indik.

619. Quoted by Herb Caen in the *San Francisco Chronicle,* May 19, 1983.

621. Thanks to Bob Engan.

624. WT is a ventriloquist.

626. From the movie *Gentlemen Prefer Blondes,* 1953.

627. SB in a lecture in San Francisco, November 1984.

634. Thanks to Oakley Hall.

637. SK is a standup comedian.

Index of Authors
Roman numerals refer to the first, second, or
third *637 Best Things Anybody Ever Said*

Index of Subjects and Key Words
Roman numerals refer to the first, second, or
third *637 Best Things Anybody Ever Said*

Thrift, II.227
Tide, III.382
Time, I.47, I.470, III.392
Timers, III.620
Titanic, III.494
Toaster, III.96
Toddling, II.609
Togetherness, II.617
Toilets, III.198
Tolstoy, III.19
Tomato, III.276
Tomorrow, III.595
Tools, III.396
Toots Shor's, I.383
Touching, III.158
Tourists, II.306
Towels, I.412
Tradition, I.622
Traffic signals, II.323
Train wreck, III.371
Tramp, II.64
Tranquility, III.628
Transsexuals, II.176
Trapeze, II.72
Travel, I.427, I.464, II.428,
   III.367–382
Triple, I.395
Tristan and Isolde, III.316–317
Trophies, I.354
Trust, I.429, III.141
Truth, I.170, I.384, I.423, I.425,
   I.485, I.533, I.624, II.354,
   II.457, II.511, II.512, II.519,
   III.543, III.603
Tub, III.108
Tumescence, I.458
Tumor, III.291
Tunnel, I.483, II.300, II.498, III.406
Turkey, III.274, III.399
Turkey cocktail, II.144
Turkeys, I.86
Twin sister, III.377
Typing, II.56
Typos, II.602
Tyrants, III.164

Ugly, I.345, III.300
Ultrasuede, III.438
Unconscious, III.463
Underwear, II.178
Unemployment, III.181
Unicorn, III.109
Universe, I.22, II.1, III.394
Universities, II.360
University politics, II.130
Urologist, I.466

Vagina, II.208
Valentine, II.191
Vanity, II.364
Vasectomy, III.93
Vaughan Williams, Ralph, I.450
Vice, III.52, III.255
Vice-presidents, II.470–472
Violence, III.553
Virgin, III.86, III.134
Virgin Mary, I.12
Virginity, II.90, II.636
Virtue, I.376, I.592, III.255
Vision, III.118
Voice, III.609
Voting, II.478, II.479

Wages, II.230
Wagner, Richard, I.610,
   III.315–319
Waist, III.282
Wales, III.369
Wallet, III.201
Wallpaper, II.561
War, II.238–248, II.391, II.624,
   III.67, III.128
Warner, Jack, I.404
Warship, III.619
Washington, George, II.464
Waste, II.67
Waste of time, III.244
Water, II.137, III.584
Wax museum, III.527
Wealth, I.494, I.546, II.36, II.189
Weather, II.518, III.522

Principal Sources of Artwork

Harter's Picture Archives for Collage and Illustration, edited by Jim Harter and containing over 300 nineteenth-century cuts.

Music, A Pictorial Archive of Woodcuts & Engravings, selected by Jim Harter and containing 841 illustrations.

Men, A Pictorial Archive from Nineteenth-Century Sources, selected by Jim Harter and containing 412 illustrations.

Women, A Pictorial Archive from Nineteenth-Century Sources, selected by Jim Harter and containing 391 illustrations.

Picture Sourcebook for Collage and Decoupage, edited by Edmund V. Gillon, Jr., and containing over 300 illustrations.

The above five titles are published by Dover Publications.